P. J. Albright.

LeRoy Myers

# TWICE-BORN MEN
## *A Clinic in Regeneration*

# TWICE-BORN MEN

## A Clinic in Regeneration

A FOOTNOTE IN NARRATIVE
TO
PROFESSOR WILLIAM JAMES'S
"THE VARIETIES OF RELIGIOUS EXPERIENCE"

By

## HAROLD BEGBIE

Author of
*"The Vigil," "Tables of Stone,"*
*&c., &c.*

CINCINNATI: JENNINGS & GRAHAM

NEW YORK: EATON & MAINS

TO

# WILLIAM JAMES

PROFESSOR OF PHILOSOPHY AT HARVARD UNIVERSITY

WITH ADMIRATION AND RESPECT

*"No heart is pure that is not passionate,
No virtue is safe that is not enthusiastic."*

SEELEY.

# CONTENTS

# 8 CONTENTS

## VI

## VII

## VIII

## IX

## X

# PREFACE

## I

WHILE I was gathering together the strange and almost inconceivable materials which go to make this book, I was conscious of so many and such diverse emotions that the point of view from which it should be written changed with every fresh turn in my journey of discovery, and perplexed me increasingly with the multitude of its aspects.

But now that I sit down actually to write what I have learned, now that I set out to play showman, dramatist, or author to the little group of human beings with whom I have been companioned for the past few weeks, there is in my mind one uppermost feeling, one central and dominating sensation of the emotions, and this is a feeling of astonishment that all the terrible tragedy, all the infinite pathos, all the amazing psychology, all the agony and bitter suffering, all the depth and profundity of spiritual experience with which I have to deal, all of it, was discovered in a single quarter of London.

Here in this little book, which tells the story of

a few humble and quite commonplace human beings, is such astonishing psychology as must surely bewilder the metaphysician, the social reformer, the criminologist, the theologian, and the philosopher; and it is unearthed, brought to the surface of observation, this incredible psychology, from a single quarter of the city, from a few shabby streets huddled together on the western edge of the metropolis, forming a locality of their own, calling themselves by a particular name, and living almost as entirely aloof from the rest of London as Cranford from Drumble.

One would say that a man might go here and there in London, picking and choosing among all the city's multifarious districts, and at the end of his researches find half a dozen human beings whose psychological experiences would amaze the general world and prove of considerable, even of lasting interest to metaphysics and philosophy. But who would say that one might find, without difficulty and without selection, in a single negligible fragment of the vast city, men whose feelings, struggles, and experiences in the moral sphere contribute such extraordinary material to psychology as that of which this book is composed? One is startled by the possibility that every single individual among the city's swarming millions, the fermentation of whose brains is the spirit, mystery, and attraction of the great city, has this supreme interest for the rest of us—

that every single individual maintains a struggle
of some kind with the forces of good and evil,
and in the silence of his soul holds some secret
intercourse with the universe.   Is it possible that
the vilest, the most degraded, the most abandoned,
and even the most stupid of all those massed and
congregated millions, hides from the gaze of his
fellow-men longings and hungering aspirations
which in the eyes of the angels entitle him to his
place in the cosmos?

One feels, standing at some central point in
London, and studying the incessant multitude of
human beings, that personality is blurred into
some such sameness as one sees in a flock of
sheep, or in a procession of waves, or in an ant-
heap.   And passing through a dreary street of
interminable villas, one feels that a monotony
similar to the bricks and slates and window-
frames must characterize the lives of their occu-
piers, that the man who lives in Number 3 can be
of no more interest to us than the man who pays
the rent of Number 27, and that all the children
playing on the pavements or shouting in the road
are similar one to the other as the leaves on the
stunted limes behind the garden railings.

But reflection tells us that every human unit in
this great mass of mortality has a silence and a
solitude proper to himself alone.   His thought is
separate.   Fractional may be his occupation or
his idleness, his virtue or his vice, his laughter

or his tears; but he himself, he in the silence and
solitude of his thought, the quintessence of the
man, is integral. One may classify him in a hundred ways, and find that he fits perfectly into our
tables of anthropological statistics; but the silence
and the solitude in which his thought dwells preserve the ultimate reality of his identity from our
research.

Possibly, then, every individual life apparently
merged and lost in the thick density of the mass,
could we penetrate to this solitude of the soul,
would possess interest for the gossip and information for the student of human nature.

More or less interest; more or less information.

Yes; this is probably true. The apprehension
that every unit in the multitude has his own individual silence of the soul, his own impenetrable
chamber of thought, his own unbroken and in-
communicable solitude, brings home to us the
knowledge that one's own pressing sense of personal identity is the property of all mankind, that
sameness is ultimately impossible, that variation
is the law, that the swarm is composed of separate
and individual *ones*.

And yet it still remains remarkable that all the
wonderful biography of this book was discovered
in a single quarter of the town.

## II

In *The Varieties of Religious Experience*, Professor William James defines religion as " the feelings, acts, and experiences of individual men in their solitude, so far as they apprehend themselves to stand in relation to whatever they may consider the divine." This definition must not be restricted to theologians and philosophers. Hamlet's religion is more to humanity than that of Athanasius. The religion of Crainquebille has its profound interest. Every man who thinks at all, however noisy his public worship of the no-God, does in his solitude feel himself to stand in some relation to the universe. Every man has a religion.

This religion of the ordinary man must possess more interest for the student of human nature than " the second-hand religious life " of the conventional formalist. It has the attraction of diversity, the sympathy of drama, the force of reality. It is " the primordial thing." " Churches," says Professor James, " when once established, live at second-hand upon tradition, but the *founders* of every Church owed their power originally to the fact of their direct personal communion with the divine. Not only the superhuman founders, the Christ, the Buddha, Mahomet, but all the originators of Christian sects have been in this case."

Here, in this book, then, is a record of individual religion manifesting itself in modern London among men with whom a theologian would scarcely pause for a moment's discussion, but who may seem to the reader, nevertheless, of that very order of simple souls chosen by the Light of the World for the central revolution of human history.

If there is aught in these men to shock our respect for the normal, let it be remembered that profound changes in character are not conventional. You cannot have upheaval with platitude.

Professor James teaches the student of psychology to expect something exceptional and eccentric in men who have suffered a profound spiritual experience. He contrasts such men with the ordinary religious believer " who follows the conventional observances of his country, whether it be Buddhist, Christian, or Mohammedan; his religion has been made for him by others, communicated to him by tradition, determined to fixed forms by imitation, and retained by habit." He declares that it profits us little to study this second-hand religious life, and says, " We must make search rather for the original experiences which were the pattern-setters to all this mass of suggested feeling and imitated conduct. These experiences we can only find in individuals for whom religion exists not as a dull habit, but as an acute fever rather." As Seeley says in the phrase which I have taken for the motto of this book, " No heart is pure that is not passionate; no virtue is safe that is not enthusiastic."

Such religion as this book will contain is the strange, individual, and elemental force which one finds in the Book of Job, in the Psalms of David, in the *Pilgrim's Progress*. It is the struggle of over-mastered and defeated souls for liberty, for life, for escape from hell. It reveals in the hearts of men whom science and law would condemn as hopeless of reformation, such possibilities of purity and devotion as La Rochefoucauld would have us believe do not exist even in the hearts of the best. It is religion terribly real in men who have terribly suffered.

From this religion of my book flows everything else.

## III

At the beginning is the revelation that the lost can be saved. One listens too willingly nowadays to the pathologist ready to pronounce physiological judgment upon every soul of man. It is our avoidance of the miracle which disposes us to the conviction that certain people are beyond the reach of regeneration. Our fashionable support of the Salvation Army is inspired largely by the success of what is called its " Social Work." We think that a tramp may be lifted from the gutters, stood upon his feet, put to some task, and made a citizen; we think that a family sinking towards destitution may be emigrated to Canada and saved to human society; but, antipathy to the miracle will not let us believe that a dipsomaniac of a sudden can lose all desire for alcohol, that a criminal who has spent the best part of his life in prisons may of a sudden turn from his crime; we are sceptical about these revolutions which pathology is inclined to pronounce impossible, and as for " conversions "—as for the dipsomaniac and the gaol-bird becoming savers of other men in the name of religion—as for this, we shrug our shoulders and inquire, Is it true? or dismiss it as hysteria.

But to make a tramp a workman is commonplace. Why are we interested in dull things? To convert the worst of men into a saint is a miracle in psychology. Why are we not interested in this great matter?

### IV

What is " conversion "?

According to Professor James, in whose steps we follow with admiration and respect, " to be converted, to be regenerated, to receive grace, to experience religion, to gain assurance, are so many phrases which denote the process, gradual or sudden, by which a self hitherto divided, and

consciously wrong, inferior, and unhappy, becomes unified and consciously right, superior, and
happy, in consequence of its firmer hold upon
religious realities."

Elsewhere he speaks of "those striking in-
stantaneous instances of which Saint Paul's is the
most eminent, and in which often, amid tremendous emotional excitement or perturbation of the
senses, a complete division is established in the
twinkling of an eye between the old life and the
new."

These definitions, as all the world knows, are
illustrated in Professor James's book by remarkable and well-authenticated histories of personal
conversion. The evidence for the reality of these
immense changes in character is overwhelming,
and the only point where the psychologists find
themselves at issue is the means by which they
have been accomplished. As to that interesting
conflict of opinion the reader is referred to the
combatants. The purpose of this book, which I
venture to describe as a footnote in narrative to
Professor James's famous work, is to bring home
to men's minds this fact concerning conversion,
that, whatever it may be, *conversion is the only
means by which a radically bad person can be
changed into a radically good person*.

Whatever we may think of the phenomenon
itself, the fact stands clear and unassailable that
by this thing called conversion, men consciously

wrong, inferior, and unhappy become consciously
right, superior, and happy.  It produces not a
change, but a revolution in character.  It does
not alter, it creates a new personality.  The
phrase " a new birth " is not a rhetorical hyper-
bole, but a fact of the physical kingdom.  Men,
who have been irretrievably bad, and under conversion have become ardent savers of the lost,
tell us, with all the pathetic emphasis of their
inexpressible and impenetrable discovery, that in
the change which overcame them they were conscious of being " born again."   To them, and we
can go to no other authorities, this tremendous
revolution in personality signifies a new birth.   It
transforms Goneril into Cordelia, Caliban into
Ariel, Saul of Tarsus into Paul the apostle.

There is no medicine, no Act of Parliament, no
moral treatise, and no invention of philanthropy
which can transform a man radically bad into a
man radically good.   If the State, burdened and
shackled by its horde of outcasts and sinners,
would march freely and efficiently to its goal, it
must be at the hands of religion that relief is
sought.   Only religion can perform the miracle
which will convert the burden into assistance.
There is nothing else; there can be nothing else.
Science despairs of these people and pronounces
them " hopeless " and " incurable."   Politicians
find themselves at the end of their resources.
Philanthropy begins to wonder whether its char-

ity could not be turned into a more fertile channel. The law speaks of " criminal classes." It
is only religion that is not in despair about this
mass of profitless evil dragging at the heels of
progress—the religion which still believes in
miracle.

Professor James, you notice, speaks of men
consciously *unhappy* becoming consciously *happy.*
This phrase helps one to understand that particular side of the Salvation Army's methods which
offends so many people—its bands, its cheerful
singing, and its laughing optimism. You cannot
imagine what effect these exhilarating bands,
these rejoicing hymns, and these radiant Salvationists produce in streets of infinite squalor and
abysmal degradation. Think what it means for
a sodden and degraded Miserable, shivering some
Sunday morning in his filthy rags on the steps
of a common lodging-house, hating himself, hating God, and regarding the whole race of humanity with hostility, to hear suddenly the jocund
clash of brass music, to catch words that challenge
his wretchedness and despair with exhilarating
joy, and then to see among those marching down
the centre of his dreary street, happy, clean, and
rejoicing, the very men who once shared his dog's
life of misery and crime.

It is the rejoicing, singing, irrepressible happiness of the Salvationist, which often makes him
such a powerful saver of other men. Such a

spirit exists in these savers of the lost as moved
an American writer, quoted by Professor James,
to exclaim: " I am bold to say that the work of
God in the conversion of one soul, considered
together with the source, foundation, and pur-
chase of it, and also the benefit and eternal issue
of it, is a more glorious work of God than the
creation of the whole material universe." Such
a phrase almost disgusts the cold-blooded. But
at the very heart of this mystery of conversion is
a wild joy. A soul consciously unhappy has become consciously happy. A soul bound and in
prison has been loosed and is free. Does one
expect a man whose entire being has suffered so
great, so pervasive, so cataclysmic a change, to
walk sedately, to measure his words, to take the
temperature of his enthusiasm and feel the pulse
of his transport? The enchanted felicity which
sends this man singing and marching into the
slums is not only the token of the miracle in
himself, but is the magic, as my book shows over
and over again, which draws unhappy and dejected souls to make surrender of their sin and
wretchedness.

Does not Christ speak of a sinner's repentance
actually *increasing* the joy of Heaven?

I have walked with one of these converted
Salvationists—an ex-soldier and now a road-
labourer *—through some of the most evil and

* " The Tight Handful," p. 63.

desperate streets in West London. I observed
how his handsome face, with its bronzed colour
and its bright eyes, the proud carriage of his
vigorous body, and the steadied cheerfulness of
his voice, attracted the notice and held the attention of the hundreds of disreputable people
swarming in that neighbourhood. I attributed
this interest to his good looks and his air of well-
being; for my companion, on these occasions, was
not in the uniform of the Salvation Army; fresh
from his work, fresh from his tea in a comfortable and happy home, well dressed, smart, and
attractive, he walked as an English workman,
consciously right, superior, and happy, through
streets filled with people consciously wrong, inferior, and unhappy. But I discovered the
reason for the attention he attracted. I said that
the people seemed to regard him with wonder,
and a little envy. "You should see them," he
replied, "when we march down here on Sunday
morning in the red jersey; I, Tom This, Joe
That, and Will Otherfellow, all of us at one time
the worst men in the whole neighbourhood."

The joy of the converted Salvationist, so attractive and startling to miserable and abandoned
wretches, is an essential feature of reform by
conversion. It is almost the central force of
the whole movement. But it, in its turn, effects
conversion by love of the highest order—love
which seeks out the lost and shows infinite tender-

ness to the worst. Professor James has not missed this feature of work by conversion. "General Booth, the founder of the Salvation Army," he says, "considers that the first vital step in saving outcasts consists in making them feel that some decent human being cares enough for them to take an interest in the question whether they are to rise or sink." The amazing work accomplished by the Salvation Army—a work which I think is only now in its infancy, and which will probably be subjected to endless evolutionary changes without losing its essential character—is a work of Love fired and inspired by Joy.

If psychologists would know the secret of this miracle, working now in almost every country under the sun, they will find that it lies in using men once consciously wrong, inferior, and unhappy, using them to seek and to save, with a contagious joy and a vital affection, those of their own condition in life who are still consciously wrong, inferior, and unhappy, and who are thus in despair about themselves only because they believe that no one on earth or in heaven cares whether they rise or sink.

The social work of the Salvation Army is as nothing to its spiritual work, and that social work itself could not exist without the miracle of conversion.

## V

This psychological mystery of conversion deserves the practical attention of the social reformer.

In this book it will be seen that all the punishments invented by law for the protection of property and the reformation of the criminal, fail absolutely of their purpose in certain cases, and only render more hard and more rebellious the lawless mind; whereas that lawless mind, apparently so brutal, terrible, and hopeless, responds with extraordinary sensitiveness to love and pity, and under the influence of religion becomes perfected in all that makes for the highest citizenship.

It would be a simple reform, and yet one of the most humane and useful, if the State did away with the formality of prison chaplains, men who too often perform their perfunctory duties with little enthusiasm and with little hope of achieving anything, and admitted, under proper authority, some such organization as the Salvation Army, which has in its ranks many men who have themselves suffered in prison, who know the criminal mind, and who would approach the most deplorable and hopeless case with the certain knowledge that conversion is possible.

Few people, I think, after reading this book, will be able to enunciate the prayer, " That it may please Thee to have pity upon all prisoners and captives," without feeling that divine pity will only manifest itself when human pity has learned to make use of common sense in the matter of its State prisons.

The strange revelations which this book makes concerning our prisons and our police, while they must shock and surprise the reader, will lead, I hope, to some change in administration which will prevent the manufacture of a *criminal class*—one of the achievements of the present system.

The police have many virtues, the prison system has of late years been greatly improved, but, as this book will show, for certain men, forming what is called the criminal class, police and prison join forces to build a barrier against their improvement. It is appalling to think that men who once got into the black books of the police of their neighbourhood, were marked down by them for such cruel harassing, such fiendish persecution, and such cowardly bullying as hardly disgraced a man-o'-war in the worst days of the press-gang.

However this particular attitude of the police towards their enemies may have changed of late, for masses of people in London the police still exist, not as the guardians of public order, but as agents of the rich and enemies of the poor.

Until one penetrates into the vast areas of destitution which crowd on every side the little centre of London's wealth and prosperity, it is impossible to realize how largely this barbarous notion of the police rules the minds of the multitude. Few things so sharply challenge our civilization deeply reflected on as this attitude of the poor towards the guardians of public order.

## VI

While it is impossible for one to say, after reading the strange histories recorded in this volume, that any man is hopelessly lost to religion, virtue, and self-respect, the ancient conviction remains—a form of the adage which says, Prevention is better than Cure—that the business of all reformation begins with the child.

In the first pages of this book I shall attempt to sketch the neighbourhood in which I made the acquaintance of my broken earthenware. London is made up of such localities, few, perhaps, worse, many as bad, but all marked by the one great damning shame of child waste. Wherever you go in London you will find children living under the horrible influence of parents who deny, with every commandment in the Decalogue, the authority of the moral sense and the commonest laws of sanitation. To leave these children under the domination of such parents is to imperil their physical and moral well-being, is to bring up a posterity unworthy of a proud and high-spirited nation, is to lay upon our children an increase of that burden which is already causing us to stumble in our march.

"One million people are living on the rate-payers," says a newspaper. "Twenty-six millions of money are raised in one way or another to support this host of paupers." The Salvation Army speaks of "the vast army—numbering tens of thousands—of tramps who prey on the public charity to the estimated extent of three millions a year, who do no work, and who cost the community an immense sum in Poor Law relief."

Is the burden being lightened or increased? Is it likely to lighten or decrease while the children of the slums are left with their abominable parents?

There is another aspect. Is it humane, has it the sanction of the religious conscience of the nation, that children should be left to live with parents infinitely below the moral standard which exists among the negroes of Africa?

We have ceased to be sentimental. Such a ballad as *The Cry of the Children* would fail to move the contemporary world. But we are practical, we are anxious to do well. Some appeal addressed to the religious conscience of the nation in the name of this great army of soiled innocence and poisoned childhood—*if it showed a practical way out*—would surely meet with a response. The Churches, who have divine reasons for conserving the purity of the child, and politicians, whose responsibility to posterity *is* the child, must feel if they give attention to this subject that the necessity for immediate and drastic action is at our doors.

In the meantime there is appalling waste, hideous ruin, and unthinkable pain. One reads, for instance: " Turn to any town, and you find the officials saying, ' There are scores of little children in this town—nay (where the town is a large one) hundreds—living under circumstances of the most shocking depravity: living in conditions from which, under existing Acts of Parliament, they ought to be rescued; living in surroundings in which it is impossible for them to grow up other than a burden and a danger to the State: living in a manner which makes them a source of moral defilement to all other children with whom they come in contact, whether at school or elsewhere: living in what are nothing else than human middens.' "

At a low estimate the children of the worst tramps number five thousand, a fragment of the army of childhood doomed to unspeakable suffering and corruption from their infancy; in Great Britain there are thirty thousand children " doomed to be criminals, doomed to be outcasts, to be even worse than that."

## VII

Beyond seeking to interest the reader in the psychological mystery of conversion, and beyond seeking to bring home to practical men the immense value of personal religion in the work of social regeneration, that is to say, in the work of developing national character, this book endeavours to create sympathy for two rational and economic reforms: a reform of our prison system, especially in its educative and saving functions; and a reform of our administration as touching the children of iniquitous parents.

The note of the book is not one of despair; it is distinctly one of hope. That is why action is so reasonable and so compelling.

# I

# A PART OF LONDON

A TURNING from one of the great main
roads on the western side of London
brings you into a district which is chiefly
famous for containing some of the worst streets,
and some of the lowest characters, known to the
police. The residents of this neighbourhood will
point out to you, with local pride, the public-
house frequented by Milsom and Fowler before
their terrible murder in Muswell Hill.

You would never suspect, while you pass down
the main road, the existence of so deplorable a
quarter. On either side of you are some of the
finest private houses in London; the traffic of
carriages and automobiles is incessant; the pavements are vivid and animated with a ceaseless
procession of humanity; and everywhere one sees
that flagrant exhibition of great wealth which
almost frightens those who know the destitution
of the poor. Presently the private houses end,
and shops begin. In the midst of these shops,
which are not of the first class, stands a station
of the Underground Railway. Here there is
noise, smell, and shabbiness. Motor omnibuses,
panting and vibrating, are drawn up at the kerb;

dirty and ragged newspaper lads toss for pennies
and discuss horse-races; flower-girls, with the
leather straps of their baskets depressing their
shoulders, exhibit bright flowers, whose contrast
to their human ugliness is complete; under the
glass porch of the railway station there is always
a crowd of people waiting for an omnibus or a
friend; and the traffic just here is heavy, noisy,
and continuous, for this point is the junction
of several roads.

The pavement is strewn with dust, dirt, and
refuse. You tread upon a carpet of omnibus
tickets, scraps of newspaper, cigarette ends,
matches, tissue paper from oranges, hairpins, and
that inevitable chaff of the London streets, composed of broken straw, hay, and dust, which the
lightest wind can lift and blow into the eyes of
pedestrians.

Disagreeable as this busy corner is, and that in
many ways, one still sees on every side women
extravagantly dressed, men of fashion, and a
tide of pleasure traffic which suggests nothing
but wealth, ease, and festivity.

But with one step you are out of this cheerful
vulgar world.

The quarter of London which we are about to
penetrate is approached from the thronging pavements of the main thoroughfare by a road even
more densely packed. It is the market street of
the Miserables. The shops are faced by an un-

broken line of stalls at the kerb's edge. Between
the darkened windows of the shops and the bril-
liant stalls of the gutter, passes a swarm of very
dirty and brutal-looking people, mostly women,
the coppers of whose greasy purses, acquired by
sin and crime, are eagerly sought by the hoarse-
voiced stall-holders.

Apparently the tradesmen who pay rent and
rates have nothing to do but stand desolately at
their shop-doors, and watch the thriving business
of their more than opposite neighbours. Among
these stalls, where you can buy the best straw-
berries for three-halfpence a pound, meat and
fish for a few pence, corsets, caps, and shoes for
next to nothing, one observes with some astonishment cut flowers and flowers in pots, pictures,
and books. Is it not wonderful that the very
poor buy flowers, and books, and pictures? It is
also interesting to notice that while the customer
stands in front of the fruit and vegetable, or
fish and meat stall, making a bargain, the whole-
sale merchant, in his smart pony and trap, is at
the back waiting to do business with the retailer.
The commerce of the great city, flowing in from
all the seas of the world, has these strange and
numerous backwaters.

At the end of this busy road, terminated by
several public-houses, one comes into the private
quarter of the neighbourhood. Here you find
almost every kind of house except the best. You

find the large and comfortable villa, once re-
splendent with the new paint and flower-boxes
dear to the prosperous citizen, and the straight
line of neat, low, one-storied houses dear to the
working man.   All are now shabby, all are now
stricken with misery.   The large villa is occupied
by some more or less respectable workman, who
lives in the basement and lets off the other floors.
The front gardent is uncultivated.   The pavements and roadway are filled with shouting children, who chalk wickets on garden walls, and lines
for hop-scotch on the pavement.   Many of these
children, the great majority, are wonderfully well
clothed, beautifully clean, and appear far more
happy and vigorous than their anæmic contemporaries of Kensington Gardens.   At one of these
houses, rented and occupied in the basement by
a Salvationist, as many as seventy beggars have
called from the neighbouring street in a single
week.

One turns out of these respectable streets,
where the children are playing cricket, cherry-
bobs, hop-scotch, hoops, and cards, and suddenly
finds oneself in streets miserable and evil beyond
description.

These are streets of once decent two-storied
villas, now lodging-houses.  The very atmosphere
is different.   One is conscious first of dejection,
then of some hideous and abysmal degradation.
It is not only the people who make this impres-

sion on one's mind, but the houses themselves.
Dear God, the very houses seem accursed! The
bricks are crusted, and in a dull fashion shiny
with grime; the doors, window-frames, and railings are dark with dirt only disturbed by fresh
accretions; the flights of steps leading up to the
front doors, under their foul porches, are worn,
broken, and greasy; the doors and windows in the
reeking basements have been smashed up in nearly
every case for firewood—again and again one sees
the window-space rough-boarded by some landlord anxious to preserve his property from the
rain. Here and there a rod is missing from the
iron railings—it has been twisted out and used
as a weapon.

In these streets, on a summer evening, you find
the flights of steps occupied by the lodgers, and
the pavements and roadways swarming with their
children. The men are thieves, begging-letter
writers, pickpockets, bookmaker's touts, totters
(rag and bone men), and trouncers (men paid by
costermongers to shout their wares), and bullies.
The women add to their common degradation—
which may be imagined—the arts of the pick-
pocket, the beggar, the shoplifter, and the
bully.

A drunken man, who wakes up to find himself
in one of these houses, is given a few old rags
wherein to make his return home, but his purse,
his watch, his pocket-book, and his papers are not

more tenaciously claimed by his terrible host than every shred of his clothing.

Sunday morning witnesses the strangest sight in these streets. The lodgers hold a bazaar. From end to end the railings are hung with fusty and almost moving rags, the refuse of the week's picking and stealing, which no pawnbroker can be brought to buy. Neighbours, barely dressed, many of them with black eyes, bandaged heads, and broken mouths, turn out to inspect this frightful collection of rags. There is bargaining, buying, and exchanging. Practically naked children look on, and learn the tricks of the trade.

If you could see these bareheaded women, with their hanging hair, their ferocious eyes, their brutal mouths; if you could see them there, half-dressed, and that in a draggle-tailed slovenliness incomparably horrible; and if you could hear the appalling language loading their hoarse voices, and from their phrases receive into your mind some impression of their modes of thought, you would say that human nature, in the earliest and most barbarous of its evolutionary changes, had never, could never, have been like this; that these people are moving on in a line of their own, that they have produced something definitely non-human, which is as distinct from humanity as the anthropoid ape. Ruth, or even Mary of Magdala, at the beginning of the line; two thousand years of progress; and then these corrupt and mangy things at the end! This is not to be believed. No; they do not belong to the advancing line, they have never been human. For the honour of humanity, one rejects them.

Concerning the men, one thing only need be said. Every woman—the oldest hag amongst them—challenged me with a hating stare, the boldness and effrontery of which struck me more than the enmity; every man seemed to be ashamed. There was cunning in their faces, there was every expression of stealth and underhand craft, but they looked and lowered their eyes. I was more impressed by this apparent shamefacedness of the men than by the murderous hostility of the women. They seemed to me " consciously wrong, inferior, and unhappy."

But more than by anything concerning the men and women of this neighbourhood, one is impressed by the swarm of dreggy children playing their poor little pavement games in the shadow of these lodging-houses. Some—can it be believed?—are decently clothed and look as if they are sometimes washed; degraded mothers, sitting on the door-steps, may be seen proudly exhibiting a baby to their friends, cooing over it, brushing its poor little pale cheeks with a black finger, suddenly stooping their foul faces to cover the little mouth with gay and laughing kisses; one of my first experiences in these streets was to hear the sudden opening of a top-story window, to see a frightful woman thrust herself half out, and to hear her shout to a toddling child to come out of the road and on to the pavement—although not a cart of any kind was in view; but this sentimental affection of the mother does not last very far beyond the period of helpless infancy. The mass of these children above five or six years of age are terribly neglected. I have never seen children more dirty, more foully clothed, more dejected-looking. In all cases, to use a phrase which I am told is common in the district, these poor children are "lousy as a cuckoo." I saw many children with sores and boils; I also saw some children whose eyes looked out at me from a face that was nothing but a scab.

A mortuary chapel has had to be built for this neighbourhood. The rooms of the houses are so crowded that directly a person dies the body must be moved.

Can the boys of these dreadful streets grow into anything but hooligans, or the girls do anything but earn money in their mothers' fashion?

Let me put the common question, but with real emphasis: Would we allow a dog to live in these streets?

Well, into these streets come day after day, and every Sunday, the little vigorous corps of the Salvation Army stationed in this quarter of London. The adjutant of this corps some years ago was a beautiful and delicate girl. She prayed at the bedside of dying men and women in these lodging-houses; she taught children to pray; she went into public-houses and persuaded the violent blackguards of the town to come away; she pleaded with the most desperate women at street corners; she preached in the open streets on Sundays; she stood guard over the doors of men mad for drink and refused to let them out.*

It is to the work of this wonderful woman—so gracious, so modest, and so sweet—that one may trace the miracles whose histories are contained in the following pages. The energy, resolution, and splendid cheerfulness of the present corps—some of them her own personal converts—may likewise be traced to her influence. She has left in these foul streets the fragrance of her personality, a fragrance of the lilies of a pure soul.

"Ah!" exclaimed an old gaol-bird, showing me the photograph of this woman; "if anybody goes to heaven, it'll be that there little angel of God."

They call her the angel-adjutant.

---

* On one occasion this little woman was walking home through evil streets after midnight, when a drunken man asked her if he might travel by her side. After going some way the man said: "No, you aren't afraid"; and then he mumbled to himself—"Never insults the likes of you, because you care for the likes of us."

## II

## THE PUNCHER

WHAT strikes one most in the appearance of this short, broad-shouldered, red-haired prize-fighter is the extreme refinement of his features. His face is pale, with that almost transparent pallor of the red-haired; the expression is weary, heavy, and careworn; the features are small, delicate, and regular; one cannot believe that the light-coloured eyes have been hammered, and the small, almost girlish mouth rattled with blows; he might be a poet, the last rôle one would ascribe to him is that of the ring.

Of all the men in this little group of the " saved," he is the saddest, quietest, and most restrained. He is the least communicative, too; one has to get his history more from others than from himself. He speaks slowly, unwillingly, in a voice so low that one must stretch the ear to hear him; he regards one with the look of a soul that does not expect to be understood; one feels that he is carrying a burden; at times one is tempted to wonder whether he really does feel himself to be consciously right, superior, and happy.

I account for this sorrowfulness of manner, first, by the natural inexcitability of a prize-fighter's temperament, and secondly, by the profound depths of his spiritual nature, which keeps him dissatisfied with the results of his work for others.

This man, whose fame as a prize-fighter still renders him a hero of the first magnitude among his neighbours, has been the means of saving some of the worst men in the place. Unpaid by the Salvation Army, and devoting every hour of his spare time to its work, the Puncher hungers to save by the score and by the hundred. I discovered in his nature a mothering and compassionate yearning for the souls of unhappy men, the souls of men estranging themselves from God. One perceives that every man so conscious of a mission for saving, and so conscious of the appalling misery of London, must be quiet, and silent, and sorrowful.

He is the son of fairly respectable people who came gradually down and down, till their home was a loft in some mews patronized by cabmen. It was here that the consciousness of the Puncher received its first stimulus of ambition. There was in the yard, working among the cabs and horses, a young man pointed out by the denizens of that dirty place as a wonderful hero. He had fought someone in a great fight on Wormwood Scrubbs, and had beaten him to bits.

" I remember distinctly, just as if it was yes-
terday," said the reflective Puncher, speaking in
his low voice and looking sadly away from me;
" I remember distinctly the feeling that used to
come over me whenever I looked at that man.    I
don't remember life before that.    It seems to me
that I only began to live then.    And this was the
feeling.    I wanted to be like that man.    I wanted
to fight.    I wanted people to point at me, and
say: ' There's a fighting man! '    I never thought
I should be as big a man as the cock of our yard;
I only wanted to be something like him; something as near to him as strength and pluck could
carry me.    But the day came "—he added, with
a touch of pride—" when I stood up to that very
man, a bit of a boy, I was, too—and I smothered
him.    Yes; I smothered him.    Ay, and afterwards many a man bigger than him; a lot bigger."

While he was a boy, still stirred by these heroic
longings, he started out on a career of wildness
and daring.    He had all those virile, headstrong,
and daring qualities which in such a country as
Canada or South Africa would have made him a
useful member of society, but which in London
drove him into crime.    His first escapade was
stealing a duck from Regent's Park, for which
offence he made his appearance before a magistrate.    Then one day he stole several bundles
of cloth from a shop, sold them to the keeper of
a marine store, and once more, this time with the

storekeeper at his side, stood in the dock of a
police court. The storekeeper went to prison, the
boy was fined.

His animal spirits got him into trouble at
school. There was no master able to influence
his character. He was pronounced utterly un-
manageable; his temper was said to be ungovernable; the authorities said that he endangered the
lives of other boys by flinging slates about as if
he wanted to kill someone. He was turned out
of nearly every school in Marylebone.

He was still a boy when he stole a bottle of rum
from a grocer's barrow, shared it with some of
his mates, and made himself so hopelessly drunk
that he fell into Regent's Canal. At the age of
seventeen he was put to work. Work, it was
thought, might tame his wild spirits. Moreover,
it was necessary for him to earn bread. He became a porter at Smithfield Meat Market.

It was at this time that he began seriously to
discipline his fighting qualities. He trained under
a man whom middle-aged sportsmen will remember, the redoubtable Nobby Thorpe. In a few
months he was a hero, and a man of substance.

He fought sixteen famous fights at Wormwood
Scrubbs, and won them all. Then came a challenge to meet Eycott at the Horse and Groom
Tavern in Long Acre. In those days certain of
the public-houses patronized by sporting noble-
men had covered yards at the back of their

premises for the purpose of prize-fights. It was in one of these places that the young porter from Smithfield Market met Eycott, a rare champion. The fight went through fourteen rounds, and the Puncher was declared victor. Eycott objected to this decision. The Puncher was game, and they fought again. In three rounds he had won easily.

This victory meant not only money, but fame and the patronage of powerful men. The porter from Smithfield became the flash fighting-man, a terrible type of humanity. He swaggered with lords and shook his fist in the face of the world. He met his trainer at the " Horse and Groom," and smothered him in eight rounds. Then came fights with Shields, of Marylebone; Darkie Barton, of Battersea; Tom Woolley, of Walsall; and Bill Baxter, of Shoreditch. At some of these fights at the back of London taverns, there were as many as sixteen members of the House of Lords, in addition to many of the most famous men on the turf. When the National Sporting Club was organized, the Puncher was chosen to open it in a great fight, still remembered, with Stanton Abbott. One of his most famous encounters was with Bill Bell, of Hoxton; they fought with bare fists, on Lord de Clifford's estate in Devonshire.

The record of the Puncher is, that never once was he beaten by his own weight.

In what state was he at this period of his life?

Many times he entered the ring so drunk that the referees objected. He was one of those extraordinary men who can saturate their bodies with alcohol and perform in a condition of complete drunkenness physical feats requiring the coolest brain and the deadliest cunning. It was the very obstinacy of his body to break down under this terrible strain which ultimately plunged him into ruin.

With his pockets full of money he married, bought a laundry business, took a comfortable house, kept servants, a carriage, and a pair of horses, went to race meetings, associated as a hero with the rich and powerful, and lived a life of racket and debauchery.

His body held out. He was perfectly strong, perfectly fit. The truth is his whole system was singing with the joy of success. His brain was on fire. He felt himself capable of enormous things. He was drunk nearly every day of his life. Nothing mattered.

When he began to feel the days of his fighting drawing to a close, he looked about him for another means of earning money quickly and easily. He had not far to look. He started a racing business.

His name, so famous to the sporting world, was advertised as " A guarantee of Good Faith." Under the cloak of this name he tricked and cheated in a hundred cunning and disgraceful

ways. He became the member of a gang. A tip
was given, and with an air of mystery was
worked for all it was worth by the touts and the
prophets; the horse tipped was a certain loser.
The men who gave the tip profited by the wagers
made confidently by their friends and patrons.
The gang did well, and prospered. The Puncher's guarantee of good faith sold many a sports-
man what is called " a pup."

But suddenly some of these schemes, advancing in boldness, attracted the attention of the
police. The Puncher lost at a stroke his fame,
his popularity, his good name. He was desig-
nated a low blackguard, and fell from wealth to
poverty. His wife and her relations, who had
sunned themselves in his wealth, became scornful
and antagonistic. The Puncher felt this treatment, and it made him worse. Again and again
he went to prison; each time he came out it was
to find his wife and children sinking deeper into
poverty, and showing him a colder and a dead-
lier hatred. The old glory of an establishment
and horses had quite departed. His experience
of Dives' splendour was short-lived. Destiny
prepared for him a longer experience in the rôle
of Lazarus.

In one single year, from October, 1904, to
October, 1905, he was seventeen times convicted,
chiefly for drunkenness. His wife now left him
for the third time, determined that this should

be the last. She had done with the wretch. He
was alone in poverty with his madness, an insatiable passion for drink.

He told me something of the way in which he
obtained drink during this destitute period of his
life. He used to intimidate those of his old racing companions whom it was perfectly safe to
blackmail; he would waylay the rich and powerful, and what is called " pitch a tale "; when absolutely penniless and mad for drink, he would
march into any crowded public-houses where he
was known, and demand it. *He was never refused.*

These fighting-men, when they come down to
poverty, however weak and broken they may be,
can live in a certain fashion on the terror of their
past strength. They do not cadge; they demand.
There are plenty of publicans who themselves
give drink to these terrible men—making them
first promise that they will go away—in order
to prevent a disturbance, possibly a fight.

The Puncher lived in this way. Food had no
attraction for him, indeed, he had a feeling of
repulsion for anything in the nature of solid nourishment; everything was in drink. He was a
blazing mass of alcoholic energy. The state into
which he had sunk can only be understood by a
medical man. His body was supported by alcohol and nothing else. Try and imagine the condition of his brain.

He lived now in the common lodging-houses of which I have written—lodging-houses occupied by the lowest, most desperate, and infinitely the most loathsome creatures on the face of the earth. He found no horror in these places. He was their king. No one dared to interfere with him. He was more terrible in his rags and madness than in the days of his splendour. Murder shone in his eyes; it was a word often on his lips. If he hit a man, that man fell like a stone. The Puncher, fed by alcohol, was something that spread terror through the district. As a prize-fighter he had been an object of awe; now he was an object of fear. Then he had been a man; now he was a devil.

His brain was active and cunning in one direction—the obtaining of money for drink. He devised a hundred ways for raising the wind. This outcast in his rags was not an ordinary cadging beggar; he was a man who had known wealth and comfort; a pot or two of ale could not satisfy the fiery longings of his body. He wanted drink always and for ever. He wanted to sit at his ease, and call for drink after drink, till he slept satisfied for a little; then to wake and find more drink waiting for him.

One of his tricks brought him into collision with his wife's family. He managed to obtain a few pawn-tickets for forfeited jewellery, which was to be sold by auction. Many of the publicans in low houses deal in these tickets. The Puncher bethought him of a young relative of his wife's, who had a good situation in an office. Thither he went, and showed his tickets.

He asked for a loan of seven shillings and six-pence on one of these tickets. He said that he knew a good thing for Epsom on the following day; meant to walk there that night and back the horse if he found that his information still held good.

The money was given.

It was a great sum to him in those days, but no sooner was he out of the office than it mad-dened him by its meanness. He contrasted his miserable present with his glorious past. He cursed fate, he cursed himself. What a fool he had been to ask so little! He would go back and get more.

But first he must drink.

When the silver had gone, he went back and got gold.

He was what is called " drunk to the world " when this relation of his wife—who believed him at Epsom—came upon him unexpectedly.

The news reached his wife and children that he had begun to prey upon decent members of the family. The news of what his wife was saying of him reached the Puncher. It sank deeply into his mind, and with it he himself sank deeper into the mud.

One day the Puncher's eldest son sought him out in his low haunts. The prize-fighter loved this boy above everything on earth, except drink. He looked up and saw his son standing before him in the uniform of the Salvation Army.

" What God's foolery is this? " he demanded, and laughed.

The boy pleaded with his father. He spoke of getting back from misery to comfort, of a return from wretchedness and destitution to happiness and home-love. With all the earnestness he could command, with all the anxiety of a son to save his father, the lad pleaded with the Puncher.

The Puncher laughed.

He had one form of expression for an answer. In his rags, shame, and frightful beastliness, he looked proudly at his son, and exclaimed, " *Me! —a Salvationist!* " The contempt was complete.

That phrase haunted him and delighted him, long after the son had retired discomfited. " Me! —a Salvationist! " he kept on repeating, and every time he laughed with a rich delight. It was the first joke he had enjoyed for a year.

He got profoundly drunk, out of sheer joy, and was in trouble with the police. That night he slept in a cell at the police-court.

The next day was Sunday.

He was in his cell, tortured by thirst, mad with the rage of a caged beast, cursing God for this long Sunday of solitude and imprisonment, when suddenly he heard the noise of a band through the little grating at the top of his cell.

He considered, and knew it to be the band of the Salvation Army.

He thought of his son.

As he sat there, dwelling on all the memories evoked by the thought of his boy, he compared his wretchedness and despair with the lad's brightness and goodness, and suddenly melting into tears, vowed that he would at least make an effort to live a decent life.

He spent that Sunday striving to prepare himself for the great struggle. He endeavoured to see clearly what it would mean. The temptation to drink, he knew well, would continually assail him. The distaste for steady work, which had always characterized him, would take long to overcome. It would be a hard fight, the hardest he had ever put up, but it was worth it. Instead of the lodging-house, a home; instead of the lowest companionship, the love of wife and children; instead of the prison, security and peace! Surely, this was worth a big fight.

On the following morning he stood in the dock. There were plenty of officials to tell the magistrate the past record of this prisoner. Unfortunately there was no one to tell him what thoughts had been working in his brain all that long Sunday in the terrible solitude of the cell. The

sentence was a month's hard labour. No doubt
many people who read the case in the newspaper
said that the punishment was inadequate, and
called the Puncher hard names. One can only
judge men by written statements: the admission
of anything else is impossible. The Puncher
deserved his month.

What did that month's imprisonment do for
him in his new state of mind? It had a curious
effect upon him. It roused him into a new form
of mental energy. Braced, vigorous, and restored to something of his old glowing joy in his
strength, he looked with an equal loathing both
on his life of horror and on his intention to reform it.

His soul was filled with a vague consciousness
of some unattainable superiority which he had
missed by his past life, and which he would have
even further degraded by his notion of a reformation. Only in the deplorable condition to which
drink had reduced him, could he have entertained
the base notion of creeping back to his wife with
a plea for pity and forgiveness. He revolted from
himself. How low must he have fallen to contemplate the cowardice of repentance! God in
Heaven, to what further depths of infamous disgust might he descend, if it were possible for
him a few hours ago to think of religion!

Do you understand this condition of his mind?
He was conscious of some unattainable superi-

ority. He felt himself infinitely above his degradation, and infinitely above his pious son in the red jersey. He was conscious of a great manhood, of powers capable of inexpressible achievement, of some immense superiority just beyond his reach, and of which the world—God curse it!—had cheated him.

No; not unattainable.

It flashed upon him that it was attainable.

He could attain it by Death.

This man, whose pale and refined face tells of a profound spiritual warfare, felt himself grow to the fulness of his stature in the realization that death would save him from himself.

When he left the prison his mind was made up.

He would murder his wife, and end his life by dying gamely on the scaffold.

This intention was perfectly clear and definite in his mind. It was a fixed idea. So powerful was it, of such extraordinary power, that it utterly destroyed his mania for drink. Psychologists, interested to observe how a religious idea will suddenly uproot a long-established habit, will be equally interested to find how an idea of hate destroyed the appetite for alcohol in the body of a man literally saturated with the poison. The old-established madness was exorcised by a single idea formed in the mind during a period of enforced deprivation. One devil went out, another entered.

The Puncher went straight from the prison to some of his old sporting acquaintances. He borrowed a sovereign. He drank with his friends till he was drunk, because they pressed him, but he did not break the sovereign for drink. With this money he purchased a butcher's knife and a hamper of food. He concealed the knife on his person, and carried the provisions to his wife.

The woman, who had suffered terribly at his hands, but who had never helped him, received his advances chillingly. He proposed a reconciliation, presenting the food as his peace-offering. Then he suggested a visit to the local music-hall. Apparently out of fear of his fists, she accepted his proposal. She accepted the proposal of a man with murder in his heart, the means of murder on his person, and a man who was drunk.

The Puncher's hatred for his wife was deep-seated. Her personality jarred upon him at every point. On her, too, centred the accumulated animosity he felt for her relations, who had done so much, he considered, to break up his home. To murder her did not in the least daunt his mind; the contemplation of the act did not unnerve nor strike him as horrible; rather it seemed to him in the nature of achievement, delightful justice, getting even with all his multitudinous enemies at one stroke.

They went out from the house.

As they passed down the street, a door opened,

and a Salvationist, who knew the Puncher and knew his son, came out and joined them. He asked if husband and wife were coming to the meeting. The Puncher said, No. The Salvationist—himself a converted drunkard and wife-beater—turned and looked the prize-fighter in the face. He told him simply and straightly, looking at him as they went down the street, that he could never be happy until his soul was at peace. He said this with emphatic meaning. Then he said, " God has got a better life for you, and you know it." The Puncher struck across the road and entered a public-house. His wife waited at the door for her murderer.

He says that while he stood drinking in the bar, feeling no other emotion than annoyance at the Salvationist's interference, suddenly he saw a vision. The nature of this vision was not exalted. In a flash he saw that his wife was murdered, just as he had planned and desired; that he had died game on the scaffold, just as he had determined; the thing was done; vengeance wreaked, apotheosis attained—he had died game: he was dead, and the world was done with. All this in a flash of consciousness, and with it the despairing knowledge that he was still not at rest. Somewhere in the universe, disembodied and appallingly alone, his soul was unhappy. He knew that he was dead; he knew that the world was done with; but he was conscious, he was unhappy.

This was the vision. With it he saw the world pointing at his son, and saying, " That's young ——, whose father was hanged for murdering his mother."

A wave of shame swept over him; he came out of his vision with this sense of horror and shame drenching his thought. For the first time in all his life he was stunned by realization of his degradation and infamy. He knew himself.

How the vision came may be easily explained by subconscious mentation. He had long meditated the crime of murdering his wife, he had long brooded upon the glory of dying game; an explosion of nervous energy presented him, even as it presented Macbeth, with anticipatory realization of his thought. In other words, we know all about the mechanism of the piano; but, the musician at the keyboard? *How* did shame come to this man utterly hardened and depraved? And what, in the language of psychology, is shame? How does grey matter become ashamed of itself? How do the wires of the piano become aware of the feelings of the sonata? Moreover, there is this to be accounted for: the immediate effect of the vision.

That effect was " conversion," in other words, a re-creation of the man's entire and several fields of consciousness. And, he was drunk at the time.

Drunk as he was, he went straight out from the public-house to the hall where the Salvation Army was holding its meeting. His wife went with him. He said to her, "I'm going to join the Army." At the end of the meeting he rose from his seat, went to the penitent's form, bowed himself there, and like the man in the parable cried out that God would be merciful to him, a sinner. His wife knelt at his side.

He says that it is impossible to describe his sensations. The past dropped clear away from him. An immense weight lifted from his brain. He felt light as air. He felt clean. He felt happy. All the ancient words used to symbolize the spiritual experience of instant and complete regeneration may be employed to describe his feelings, but they all fail to convey with satisfaction to himself the immediate and delicious joy which ravished his consciousness. He cannot say what it was. All he knows is that there, at the penitent form, he was dismantled of old horror and clothed afresh in newness and joy.

Whatever the effect upon himself, the effect of this conversion on the neighbourhood was amazing. The news of it spread to every foul court and alley, to every beerhouse and gin-palace, to every coster's barrow and street corner, to every common lodging-house and cellar in all that quarter of the town. There is no hero to these people like a prize-fighter; let him come down, as the Puncher had come down, to rags, prison, and the lodging-house—still, trailing clouds of glory does he come, and the rest worship their idol even when he lies in the gutter.

When the Sunday came and this great hero marched out of barracks with the band and the banners and the lasses, there were thousands to witness the sight—a dense mass of poverty-stricken London, dazed into wonderment by a prize-fighter's soul. "The Puncher's got religion!" was the whispered amazement, and some wondered whether he had got it bad enough to last, or whether he would soon get over it and be himself again. Little boys swelled the multitude, gazing at the prize-fighter who had got religion.

He had got it badly.

His home became comfortable and happy. He appeared at all the meetings. No desire for tobacco or drink disturbed his peace or threatened his holiness. The neighbourhood saw this great fighter going every night to the Army Hall, and marching every Sunday to the meetings in the open air.

Then they saw something else.

The wonder of the Puncher is what Salvationists call his "love for souls." This is a phrase which means the intense and concentrated compassion for the unhappiness of others which visits a man who has discovered the only means of obtaining happiness. The Puncher was not content with the joy of having his own soul saved; he

wanted to save others.    He did not move away
from the neighbourhood which had witnessed his
shame, but lived there the life of a missionary.
Every hour of his spare time, every shilling he
could spare from his home, was given to saving
men with whom he had companied in every con-
ceivable baseness and misery.    This man, as other
narratives will show, has been the means of saving men apparently the most hopeless.    To this
day, working hard for his living, and with tragedy deepening in his life, he is still to be found
in that bad quarter of London, spending his time
and his money in this work of rescuing the lost.
I never met a quieter soul so set upon this bitter
and despairing task of rescue.

And hear something of what he has gone
through.

After his conversion, and when it seemed quite
certain that he would never revert, a lady set up
the Puncher and two other men with a pony and
cart, that they might become travelling green-
grocers.    The business prospered.    The prize-
fighter and ex-dandy was quite happy in his work.
Money came sufficiently for the needs of his home.
The work was hard and incessant, but it was
interesting.

Then his wife gradually cooled towards the
Army.    It was not respectable enough for her
relations.    She did not gird at her husband, but
she withheld sympathy.    Probably she wished

him to remain a Salvationist, if that meant her own immunity from his chastisement; but she would have been better pleased, from a social point of view, if the Puncher had kept his morality and sloughed his religion.

Almost more difficult to bear, the son whom he loved so greatly—the boy who had done so much to save him—resigned from the Army and gave his thoughts to other things. He did not become bad or vicious, or even indifferent to religion, but the old enthusiasm, the old energy which alone can keep a mind to this exacting form of service, vanished. The Puncher was the only Salvationist left in his home.

One bitter winter's day he was on his rounds with the pony-cart in North London. The third partner in the venture had gone out of the business. The Puncher was on this round with the other man, his only partner. " Puncher," said this man, pulling up at a public-house, " I'm going to have a nip of whisky; it's perishing cold. You come in too, and have a glass of port—port's teetotaller's drink."

The Puncher said, No. The partner wheedled and coaxed. It was cold.

" Port's teetotaller's drink," said the partner. " One glass can't hurt a man like you; come on, I'll stand it."

The Puncher fell. He was miserable, lonely, and unhappy in his home. It was cold. His partner stood in the tavern, calling him in. The Puncher followed him. He thinks that the wine was drugged. He dropped like a shot man on the floor of the public-house, and when they picked him up, and got him round, his partner had disappeared with the pony and trap. Such is one aspect of the life of London. In the City the same kind of cleverness is practised in other ways. The Puncher was still drunk when he arrived back in his own neighbourhood. People seeing him stagger through the streets did not laugh nor mock; they were genuinely sorry—even the worst of them—to see this great-hearted man fallen back into ruin. A kind of silence held the crowded streets as the Puncher with sunk head and giving legs shambled to his home, a terrible look in his eyes and jaws.

Then the tongues wagged. In a few minutes all the neighbourhood knew that the Puncher's conversion had not lasted. People talked of nothing else. They wondered if he had already wrecked his home and smashed his wife. Some of them slouched round to his street and hung about in front of his house. A crowd assembled.

The door opened. The Puncher came out. He had taken off his coat, and had put on the red jersey. He walked straight to the Army Hall, went to the penitent form, and prayed.

That was a brave thing to do. But the

Puncher does not see the courage of it. One thought stuck in his mind when he came to himself, drunk, ruined, and alone in that public-house in the North of London: the thought that he would be safe if he could get into his uniform. It was not the honour of the regiment he thought about, but the covering protection of the Flag. He went to his uniform for protection. This is a true story, and it seems to me there is nothing more remarkable in the narrative than the poor beaten fellow's fixed idea that if only he could get into his jersey he would be safe.

From that day he has never fallen. The shadows have deepened for him. His wife's lack of sympathy is an increasing distress and discomfort in the home. The solitude of his soul there is complete. His children do not care about their father's religion. He has to earn his living among men who are not Salvationists, and who do not show him sympathy. But in spite of this the Puncher remains in the neighbourhood of which I am writing, and he is there perhaps the greatest force for personal religion among the sad, the sorrowful, the broken, and the " lost " who cram its shabby streets.

" The Puncher," someone said to me, " has spent hours and pounds trying to reach his old companions. He is chiefly unhappy because he has not saved more than he has. He seems to think of nothing else. He's always talking about

it, in his quiet, low voice, and with that queer
straining look of longing in his sad eyes."

He receives no pay from the Army. He is not
an officer, he is a soldier—a volunteer. The time
he gives to the work is the time left over from an
arduous day of earning daily bread.

When I suggested to the adjutant * mentioned
in the preface, that it might be well for the Army
to deliver this remarkable man from the task of
earning his living, and set him free to " testify "
all over the kingdom, she replied:

" He testifies every now and then at great
meetings, and wherever his name appears we get
vast audiences, for he is known all over England,
especially in places where there are race-courses.
But the Army does not encourage this idea, because a man who continually narrates the story
of his evil deeds is apt to glory in them; that is a
great danger, and it is not conversion. You see,
we do not stop at converting people from crime
and wickedness, we endeavour to lead them on to
the heights of character. This man is quite lovely
in his mind. His wistfulness for the souls of
others is almost feminine; it is an intense yearning. And the discipline of earning his daily
bread is far better for him than the excitement
of continually narrating the story of the past,

* An officer devoting all his or her time to the Army's
work, and in this case in charge of a local organisation
called a corps; the corps comprising a number of soldiers.

from which he is spiritually moving every day of his brave life. I think we are wise in this. To be converted is only a new beginning of something greater."

Does not this remark of the little adjutant give one fresh ideas of the Salvation Army as a spiritual force?

# III

# A TIGHT HANDFUL

HOW does science account for this man?
His father was the best type of English soldier, a man with discipline in the blood, full of self-respect, proud of obedience, brave, upright, and orderly.

He had soldiered in the 13th Light Dragoons, now the 13th Hussars, and rode with his regiment on the right of the line at Balaclava. He was one of the six hundred who charged the Russian guns with sabres; he was one of the remnant that rode back out of the jaws of death, out of the mouth of hell. Steadier and better trooper of horse never served his country. The man was clothed with some mysterious dignity; an aloofness of self-respect which was pride in its highest manifestation showed in his manner, his appearance, and his speech. He held himself proudly, was inexorable in his duty, and only forsook taciturnity in unwilling monosyllables. He was what Carlyle would have called, a great, silent, inarticulate soul.

He left the army a hero, and became a policeman.

He was the Police Inspector of Charing Cross Station.

The home was in Deptford. It was comfortable, respectable, and religious. The children were sent in best clothes to Sunday-school, and were apprenticed to the Band of Hope. On Sunday evenings company was received. The entertainment was religious. They sang sacred songs and hymns; they discussed life from the religious standpoint. Whisky and water helped this flow of soul, the men smoked cigars in a deliberate and philosophical fashion. Many great problems were left unsolved at these discussions.

There were several quite young children in this household when the head died. The hero of Balaclava left behind him, in addition to his medals and the record of a useful life, a wife and family who needed bread for their existence." The burden of this responsibility fell upon the wife. She went out to work, and became a cloak-room attendant at Charing Cross Station. She is there to this day.

The long life of this woman's devotion is typical of London. The number of poor women who go out to work for the sake of their children, who toil from early morning to late at night, and who manage, in spite of this, to keep the home respectable and cheerful, to endear themselves to their children and permanently to influence the characters of those children towards honesty, uprightness, and self-respect, is legion. Into

whatever poor parish of the town you may enter,
the clergyman, the doctor, the district nurse, or
the local Salvationist will tell you that the best
of the inhabitants are working mothers, whose
lives are one incessant struggle for the mere necessities of existence.

With such blood in his veins, with such memories in his young heart, with such noble and
sacred influences on his soul, the hero of this
story left home at the age of fourteen to enlist
in a line regiment, of which an elder brother was
one of the colour-sergeants.

The life of a boy in the army at that time, particularly a boy in the band, was hard and cruel.
It took either a genius to dodge its hardships, or
a giant to withstand its cruelties. The private
soldier appeared to take a savage pleasure in
hardening the heart of a boy; it was the tyranny
of a lad for a cat; there was in it the element of
sport.

It seemed to my hero, from the outset, that he
must fight for his hand. He was strong, proud,
high-spirited. Moreover, his brother was a colour-sergeant. In a few weeks he was swearing, smoking, drinking, and fighting—like a
man.

At fifteen he went to Ireland; at sixteen he was
in India.

In India he was as good as any man in the
regiment.

What does this mean? It means that he was smart in his appearance, knew his drills, and could appear on parade full of beer without detection. He was famous for this ability, and he was proud of it. Much of the talk in a canteen concerns the capacity of a man to carry liquor on steady legs. It is a useful topic of conversation. It makes for pleasurable disputation, it leads to wagers, it creates exciting contests. Who can drink the most, Jack or Joe, A company or B, ours or the Shropshires? A man who can stand up to beer is a hero who will certainly stand up to shot and shell. Who fears one barrel will fear two. The fanatic says that there is no barrel without an enemy. But the soldier stands to his gun and his beer, able to pot in two senses of the phrase—a man.

But there was something in the mind of my hero which was not satisfied by beer. He does not know what it was. It manifested itself, this unrest, in several ways. For instance, he would go to the library and pore over Queen's Regulations. He wanted to pick a quarrel. He was a barrack-room lawyer. He made sure of his ground, and then " raised hell." He claimed his rights in the face of colour-sergeant, company officer, adjutant, and colonel. The trouble was, for these authorities, that the lawyer in this case was perhaps the best soldier in the regiment—exceedingly smart, handsome, energetic, and keen.

Furthermore, he was a marksman—the company shot.

But Queen's Regulations did not satisfy him any more than success at the butts, or smartness on parade, or beer. There was still something wanting. He was sufficiently educated to feel dissatisfied with the scope of his existence; there was that in his nature which made him an inquirer, a barrack-room lawyer considering the affairs of the universe—a man whose grudge was not against the service, but against life. Somewhere in the cosmos there was a person or a thing he desired to meet face to face; if necessary with naked fists.

At Conoor he fell in with a corps of the Salvation Army. The universe seemed at last to have answered his inquiries. He was conscious of a call. He used to go down to the services and prayer-meetings, always in a state of liquor, sometimes very drunk, and throw out those of the worshippers who failed to reach the standard of that which he deemed a seemly religious propriety. It was a curious condition of mind. He felt himself to be protecting the weak, championing the derided, reproving the mockers. He approved in a dull way the idea of God, and the thought of heaven and hell, the religious thesis of a struggle between good and evil. These great thoughts enlarged the boundaries of existence. They gave his soul a little more room in which to turn round, a little better air to breathe. So he stood up for the Salvation Army in barrack-room and canteen, pot in hand; he rattled those who derided it with a crackle of oaths; he was ready to fight for it.

The mystery of this state of mind can be easily explained. There is no subject in the world like religion for argument, controversy, and dispute. The Bishop of London told me that on one occasion in Victoria Park, when he was waiting to answer an atheist lecturer, a little greasy-haired man suddenly planted a box on the ground, mounted it, and exclaimed, with a pathetic anxiety to be heard, " Ladies and gents, 'alf a mo' about that ole 'umbug General Booth! " It is religion which draws the crowd of listeners to the parks; it is religion which makes every man an orator. On religion such born barrack-room lawyers as Charles Bradlaugh and the hero of this story will always love to hear themselves speak till the lights go out and the silence falls.

Because he wanted to be in controversy with his fellows, because he wanted to argue and orate and show his superior knowledge, the Tight Handful became a champion of the Salvation Army. If all the regiment had been pious Christians, it is very probable that his fists and his oratory would have been at the service of atheism. But he had found a minority. This was enough. He put himself face to face with the majority, fists raised, his brain singing with beer.

He left India a very much worse man than he arrived. He was made a corporal, well on his way to lance-sergeant, and the highest warrant rank might easily have been his. But he had shipped a devil. His love of controversy had opened a door; one of the worst devils known to the student of human nature had entered; it was the devil of rage. Men truly said of him, " He has got the devil of a temper."

This story is really a study in temper. The part played by drink is quite subsidiary. The interest lies in the wild fury which grew gradually in the character of this young soldier till it became a demon uncontrollable, ungovernable—his master.

To this day his prominent cheek-bones have that glaze, and his eyes that shining fire, which are so often the outward shows of a temper quick to take flame.

On the night of his arrival in England, he went out of barracks and " forgot to return " till next morning. He was made a prisoner.

This roused the fury of his temper. It was his first crime. It meant the ruin of his career. He went before the colonel, ready to fight for his life. But he was too good a soldier to be punished. He went out from the orderly-room with the shame of a reprimand burning in his blood.

Three months afterwards he was back again, charged with striking the police. This time a serious crime. He was reduced to the ranks.

Ruin!

Consider him—quite a young man, well above the standard of his fellows in education, one of the most efficient soldiers in the regiment, a prize marksman, in appearance handsome, proud, and scornful, a man physically as perfect as any in the British Army—slim, tall, broad-shouldered, deep-chested, long-armed, with true vision, and a courage that feared nothing—one who by the exercise of a little ordinary common sense might have risen to warrant rank and in a few years retired from the service with a comfortable pension; such he was, and he found his career ruined by temper in the very dawn of his manhood. Everything lost. The whole future closed against him.

The regiment tried to do for him all that was possible. He became silverman in the officers' mess, an officer's servant, even a policeman; but every job thus found for him to mitigate the bitterness of reduction to the ranks, he threw away, one after another, in scornful bouts of headlong drunkenness.

Nothing mattered to him now. He had thrown away his chances. He kicked forethought out of his path, and went plunging deeper and deeper into the abyss.

Twice he came near to murder.

In Manchester he found himself mixed up in some sordid brawl between sailors and a public woman. Such a contempt as Shakespeare had for these creatures when they unpack their hearts, took sudden possession of The Handful. The street lamp fell upon her screeching face; her hoarse voice loaded with loathsome words struck rage out of the soldier's soul—he sprang upon her, seized her by the throat, bore her to the ground, and was throttling the poor life out of her body, when an old tramp interfered, a man who had served in The Handful's regiment many years before, and whose appeal to the honour of the regiment—this ragged old tramp's appeal to the honour of the regiment!—broke through the rage in the soldier's brain, and just saved him from murder.

Later, at Aldershot, he discovered by an accident that a girl with whom he was accustomed to associate had been seen walking with a man of another regiment. This time, not in hot blood, he deliberately plotted murder. He met the girl, walked with her, taxed her with infidelity, and then set upon her. He left her dying on the lawn, and walked back to barracks to await arrest for murder. He could hardly believe it when he learned that the girl was still living.

Soon after this he left the service. His colonel

appealed to him, argued with him, to stay on and
earn a pension.   He not only resisted these ap-
peals, but suddenly brought a charge against the
regiment concerning his kit.   A few days before
he had been served out with new things.   These
things had been taken away by the colour-sergeant.   According to a new regulation, of which
the colonel knew nothing, the kit belonged to the
soldier.   The Handful, blazing with indignation,
claimed justice.   It ended, this strange scene of a
soldier's departure from his regiment, by the
colonel drawing a cheque for six pounds, and
giving it to the ex-soldier, with apologies.   The
Handful carried the cheque to the canteen and
" blew it " in drink.   When the cab, which had
been waiting for him some hours, left the barracks
it was drawn by half the men in his company,
mostly drunk.

He became door-keeper at a public-house in
Deptford, close to his mother's home.   In a single
month he had made five appearances before his
master for being drunk on duty.   Finally, he took
off his master's clothes—that is to say, his uniform—in Deptford Broadway, threw them down,
and prepared to fight his employer.   There was a
scene.   And he left.

It would be wearisome to follow him through
all his various short-lived employments at this
period of his life.   He lost them through drink
and temper.   He could not master his appetite

for drink, and when he was censured his temper
blazed up and violence followed.

And yet there was something so likable and
commending about him that in spite of his army
record, and in spite of all his subsequent vagaries,
he was able to obtain employment as railway policeman at one of the great metropolitan stations.

It was during this employment that he met his
future wife—a little, pale, soft-voiced, delicate
blonde, with hair the colour of pale straw, and
eyes like cornflowers—one of the meekest, gen-
tlest, quietest little creatures that ever attracted the
admiration of a hot-pacing devil. On the morning of his wedding-day he went to meet some
friends at Waterloo Station, who were coming up
for the event. He met some soldiers instead.
They were men of his regiment, and his regiment
was going to South Africa. They adjourned to
a public-house, and a deal of the honeymoon
money went into the pockets of brewery share-
holders. The wedding was in Marylebone at
eleven; the bridegroom arrived at 12:30, so drunk
that it was noticeable. After the service the
clergyman advised the poor little timid blonde to
take her husband home and reform him.

Some few months afterwards, while his experience of a home and domestic happiness was
still quite fresh, and when the time that he would
become a father was approaching, he was drunk
on duty. A man occupying the rank of his

father, an inspector of police, rebuked him and ordered him off duty. The Handful knocked him down with a blow in the face.

He arrived home that night in a cab, suspended from duty. It was after midnight, nearly one o'clock. He pulled his wife out of bed, made her dress, and took her out in the streets. There he forced her to walk up and down with him till four o'clock, when some particularly obliging public-houses open their doors. He was like a madman.

A fortnight after his son was born.

It was now that the devil of rage began to possess his whole nature and to rule every minute of his day. Hitherto there had been spells of gentleness, interludes of cheerfulness, in which he played the part of a merry and roystering companion; but now a settled sullenness, a brooding wrath, a simmering exasperation occupied his soul; he felt the blood boiling, the gorge rising, always.

He was at enmity with the whole world, his violent resentment was for life itself; but there was in his dark and wrathful mind one particular and individual animosity—it was for his wife.

In the phrase of the street, this poor little woman " got on his nerves."

As he looks back upon that time, shamefacedly enough, and yet with a certain intelligent interest of inquiry, he comes to the conclusion that it was the exceeding meekness of his wife which filled him with this irrational hate. She never complained of his drunkenness or his idleness; she never replied to his taunts; she never accused him of the suffering he had brought upon her and their child. Very quietly, this little pale-haired woman, who unlike most of her class in England is a skilful cook and an excellent housekeeper, performed the domestic duties with devotion, and kept the home together as well as she could.

It was this mildness of her disposition that exasperated the young husband.

He longed, he tells me, longed with all the fury of his brain, to see rebellion flash from her eyes, to hear bitter words pour from her lips, to feel the blow of her fist in his face. Then he might have emptied all the black displeasure of his heart in one great excusable thrashing which would have made him her master, and her his dog.

But her meekness cowered him with the feeling of inferiority.

With hate and murder in his heart he made a hell of that little home. His wife says to me, as she bends over her cake-tins in the kitchen of their basement home, " He was just like a madman." She does not look up from her work; there is no energy in her words; she would say in exactly the same tone of voice, " He was not very well," or, " The weather is trying." And the young husband, sitting on the foot of a sofa occupied by their baby at the other end, laughs quietly, stretches his long legs, and says, " I was a tight handful."

How did he treat her?

It was a curious form of tyranny. He never once laid hands upon her. " I sometimes used to wish that he would," she says quietly. No; his tyranny took another form. He held over her head a menace—the menace that he would murder her. Sometimes he would sit quietly in his chair, regard her with eyes full of hate, and say, " I'll kill you one day, mark my words! " At another time he would come smashing and swearing into the house, his face scorching red, his eyes burning, and throwing things here and there, kicking this and that out of his way, would swear by God in heaven that he could bear this woman no longer. And again, at other times, when the cry of the baby woke him from sleep and he opened his eyes to see the mother tenderly soothing the child, he would spring out of bed with an oath, and drive her from the room to spend the night— no matter how wintry—where she could. Sometimes he pursued her, on the very brink of murder. On countless occasions she spent long nights with her baby in the coal-cellar, in the little chamber which has a bolt to the door, or in the houses of neighbours, or in the streets.

The child became a cause of exasperation. He hated it almost as much as he did its mother. Again and again he was thrown into a paroxysm of fury by its little querulous cries. He longed to kill it. He had to hold himself back from seizing it up and throwing it out of the window or dashing it to the floor. He abused the mother because of the baby. He fastened upon their baby all the blinding animosity he felt for his wife. He cursed it; set his teeth, and stood over it with hands trembling in a passion of desire to throttle it. The helplessness of the child filled him with inarticulate fury. He wanted to hurt it, damage it, brutalize it. When he came back at night from the public-house, whose till he helped to load with the money of which his wife went in sore need, and found the child restless and peevish, he was flung into a fit of explosive irascibility which always ended in driving mother and child from the room, and held him in a madness of desire to murder them both and make an end of it all.

This state of things endured for three years. The woman was a Christian. All through those three years of inexpressible horror she continued to pray for the reformation of her husband. But there were times when the burden was too great for her. Twice she attempted to commit suicide.

It came to the husband, in the midst of his madness, that the hour was approaching when he would infallibly kill his wife. He lived with this thought, contemplating all that it meant—to be-

come a murderer. He became afraid of himself.
*Tel menace qui tremble*.

One night, after a storm in the house, he went
out into the streets. On his way he passed a hall
occupied by the Salvation Army. The door stood
open. A sudden impulse to enter took possession
of him. The haunted man turned from the
streets and went in.

It was the first time he had entered an Army
hall in England. They were singing happy
hymns, clapping their hands in a rhythmic, almost
mechanical, manner, with that strange abandon-
ment of joy which is so difficult for commonplace
or phlegmatic people to understand. The room
was bright and cheerful. After the hymns followed an address. It was an appeal to the
wretched, miserable, and guilty souls in the hall
to come out and publicly confess at the penitent
form their own helplessness to get right, their
need for the love and power of God.

The haunted man, afraid to what ruin this murderous hate in his heart would lead him, yielded
to the invitation. He went to the penitent form,
kneeled down, and covered his face with his hands
—waiting for the magic change in his character,
waiting to be dishaunted.

They came round him and counselled him, and
then inquired, with affectionate pressures of the
hand upon his broad shoulders, "Are you
saved?" "Do you feel that you are saved?"

He answered, " I am the same as I came in."

That night he returned home, hating himself and loathing life. When he told me this experience we were in his home, and his wife was ironing baby-linen on the kitchen table. He paused in his narration to ask her, " Where was it you slept that night, matey?—in the coal-cellar, or with neighbours? " Without pausing in her ironing, the little pale woman answered, " Oh, that night it was in the coal-cellar." The narration flowed on, the iron had not ceased its journeys over the white linen.

He was worse than ever after this effort to be saved.

At this time he was working on the Twopenny Tube, buried like a rat for long hours, and coming up to the surface at the end of a long day's work with bitterness and resentment and despair in his soul. Not an occupation likely to relieve the oppression of his mind.

Once again he turned for help to the Salvation Army. Once again he did the difficult thing of going publicly to the penitent form. And once again he experienced no relief. The blackness in his soul would not lift. He tells me that at this time there was one insistent memory of the past haunting his thoughts in the midst of a deepening despair. The first watch he ever kept in India was at the prison in Secunderabad, and while on that watch he had seen a man flogged; although at the time he was a hard, cold-blooded, and defiant young dare-devil, the sight of that flogging so took effect upon him that he almost fainted at his post. And now the terrible impression revived, a trick of the subconscious self, and he went about envying with all his heart the man who had been flogged.

He says, quite simply, but with the masterful energy of his character, " My thoughts lived with that man—if only I could get it on my back! I seemed to feel the same stripes entering my brain."

He was also haunted at this time, why he cannot say, by some words in the Bible which he had learned without comprehending their meaning, " My spirit shall not always strive with man." They frightened him.

He was conscious, in the words of Professor James, this ex-soldier, this guard opening and shutting doors on the Twopenny Tube, of being wrong, inferior, and unhappy. Is it not a holding thought to consider that some of the servants of the public in London, of whom one takes so little notice, and who appear to be such purely mechanical things in the general life, are concerned with such matters as this?—that in the solitude of their souls they feel themselves to be related to the universe, responsible to God?

The Tight Handful, with his gropings into the infinite, and the ungovernable fury of his temper,

was now going more confidently to beer for relief
than to the penitent form; going more eagerly,
and at the same time more desperately, because
it did provide him with the escape from himself
which alone averted madness and murder.

It was in a condition of drink that he returned
one day resolved to drive his wife and child out
of the house, to sell up all his furniture, and to go
himself out of London, on the tramp, anywhere
and anyhow, he cared not what might happen.
That was the revelation brought to him by drink.
He was not to worry about his soul, but to kick
responsibility out of his path, and live bravely,
defiantly, to his own pleasure. At all costs he
must escape from the deadly monotony of his
unintelligent employment, renounce all his domestic responsibilities, escape from the spiritual
hauntings which now distracted him, and taste
adventure.

What! a man with his vigour and energy and
longings, to be sunk all his days in an underground railway, to be tied to a little pale-faced
wife, to be forced to provide her with food and
clothes, and food and clothes for her baby—to
spend his days tied to this wretched go-cart of domesticity—he who had soldiered in India and
lived freely, grandly, riotously,—like a gentleman!

So he drove his wife and child from his house.
When they were gone, he found that she had

left for him, on the mantelpiece, the money for the rent, with the exception of a few shillings. This last service of faithful love steadied him a little, made him think. He went back to his duty on the railway.

And now we reach a point in the story where mystery, unaccountable to the man himself, enters and hurries the conclusion.

On his first journey that day, from the Bank to Shepherd's Bush, this young guard heard a voice. He tells you quite calmly, and with a resolution of conviction nothing can shake, that as distinctly as ever he heard sound in his life, he heard that morning a voice, which said to him: " It is your fault, not God's, that you cannot be saved; *you won't trust.*"

It was the suggestion, which psychologists perfectly understand, of surrender; the clear, emphatic injunction of Christ—the stressed idea expressed in so many forms—the absolute necessity for losing one's life, laying down one's life, losing one's soul—the new birth, being born again—almost, one might say, the *sine qua non* of Christ's revelation.

To yield, to cease to struggle, to be passive, to be as clay in the hands of the potter—utterly to surrender the will to some vast power dimly comprehended and vaguely desired—this was the instant and poignant movement in the mind of the man following the sound of the voice.

He surrendered.

"Do you know what it is," M. de Lamennais said on one occasion to his pupils, "which makes man the most suffering of all creatures? It is that he has one foot in the finite and the other in the infinite, and that he is torn asunder, not by four horses, as in the horrible old times, but between two worlds."

The whole struggle is there. It does not matter how literate or how illiterate, how great or how ignoble, how religious or how irreligious, every man according to his degree, in the solitude of his thoughts and the silence of his soul, is torn between two worlds. It is a struggle universal and inescapable. I am persuaded that even in the most abandoned and depraved of wretches this struggle never ceases; in some form or another, perverted enough in some cases, the struggle between the one world and the other goes on to the end. It really does not signify whether we call it a struggle between two worlds or between the higher and the lower natures, whether it is the immense conflict of a Hamlet or the effort of a clerk to be more industrious and honest at his duties; the significance of this duality is its universal presence in the human race, and its inexplicable insistence—unless there is a spiritual destiny for humankind. The man in this story had hated the one world because his subconsciousness was aware of the other; he had come to loathe his life because he had glimpses in the darkness of his soul of another and a better; he was consciously wrong, inferior, and unhappy, and however vaguely, however blindly, he wanted to be consciously right, superior, and happy.

Directly this complete surrender of his mind followed upon the voice, he was aware *instantly* of extraordinary peace. It was as if a typhoon had suddenly dropped to the stillness of a lake, as if a tempest of hail and snow had become instantly a summer day. And in this peace he heard not another voice, not someone from outside of him addressing his conscience, but his own inner consciousness repeating the words, " Him that cometh unto Me I will in no wise cast out."

These words, he says, repeated themselves with an unbroken iteration, so that while the train roared and shook through the darkness of the Underground he was aware of nothing else. They ceased, only to begin again. They did not set themselves to the rumble of the wheels, they blotted out all other sounds. Standing on the oscillating platform of the train between the doors of the two carriages, and penned in by the trellis gates of rattling iron, he heard these words singing and ringing in his brain with a recurrence which was not monotony, but joy, and with a meaning that was neither a menace nor a despair, but wonderful and emancipating. " I only knew," he says, " that I was saved."

The miracle had happened. Its effect was obvious immediately. In ten minutes, from the moment when he felt his soul leap suddenly into the light of understanding, he was the centre of a group of mates asking what had happened to him, so changed was his appearance. Curiously enough the humorist, who is always to be found in such crowds, put to him the question, " Have you joined the Salvation Army? " He answered, " No, mate, but I'm going to at the first opportunity, for I'm saved."

The man was completely changed. The overmastering passion for drink which had ruled him like a tyrant, the frightful rage and resentment which had made him a demon, and the disgust and hatred of life which had darkened all his outlook upon existence—vanished, ceased to exist, passed out of his life as if they had never been there.

He was filled with a delightsome joy.

Such an amazing revulsion, such a complete and total transformation of character, is an achievement possible only to religious influences. Hypnotism, as I know, can undoubtedly, after many weeks of operation, cure some men of their vices. Drugs are able in certain cases, after a long and difficult treatment, to remove the taste for alcohol. But it is only a religious force which, in the twinkling of an eye, can so alter the character of a man that he not only then and there escapes and stands utterly free from tyrannical passions, but is filled full of a great enthusiasm, desires to spend his whole life in working for righteousness, and feels as if he had fed on honey-dew and drunk the milk of Paradise.

This is the wonder-side of conversion which no theory of psychology can explain. It is also the greatest force in religion. Theology has no proofs; religious experience does not need them.

In a few days this man had found his wife, told her his story, and both were agreed to begin their life again, and to begin it by entering the Salvation Army. On the Saturday night of that week they went together to the hall occupied by the Army in the district that knew the tragedy of their former life, and at the form where twice before the young soldier had kneeled half crazed with drink and rage, they both knelt—" not to get saved," he says, " but to signify that we intended to serve God in the ranks of the Salvation Army."

That was six years ago. During those six years, this handsome and striking-looking man— as good-looking, shapely, and vigorous a man as you could wish to see—has worked for the Army without pay of any kind, has been the life and soul of his corps, and is now, with the Puncher, perhaps the greatest force making for enthusiasm in all its local activities. He does not preach, preaching is not in his line, but when he is forced to it—though the ordeal almost terrifies him—he will stand up before a crowd and " testify "— that is to say, tell of his shame and of his great deliverance. And his home, well furnished and comfortable, its shelves filled with books that he has bought for a few coppers on stalls in the gutter, is one of the happiest and most respected in all that district. He has advanced to a high place in the hard and laborious work by which he earns daily bread. There is no one among his mates, his acquaintances, or even the poor foul people of the neighbourhood, who does not respect him, think well of him, and like him. His happiness is infectious. His old mother at Charing Cross Station thanks God that she has lived to see the day of her boy's salvation.

He says to me, quite quietly, smiling and shaking his head in perplexity, " It's a fair marvel; there's no mistake about that; people can get away from a lot of things, but they can't get away from conversion. No! And see what it does for a man! It *does* give him a new birth. I've still got faults, a lot of them, but I'm absolutely different from what I was before conversion. I've got different ideas about life,—everything. I'm happy. I'm keen about helping others. I love the work, I love my home, and I can put up with a baby ! "

There is in his little sitting-room, which you would never take to be the room of a labouring man, a cabinet full of a child's old playthings, spelling-books, paint-boxes, and toy animals. It is sacred to these things. They belonged to the child he so often drove from his sight.

" I was pulled up sharp," he says, mournfully and with tears, " when the little chap went. He was eight. And I had hated him so in the bad time."

On another occasion, when we were walking through a street thronged by ragged, foul-faced, barefooted brats, about whose souls nobody appeared to care a jot, he said suddenly, " When I used to see these children, just after my boy was dead, I couldn't help wondering why he should be taken and they should be left."

Happily there is another child in the house now, and although he confesses that he is still anything but a baby's man, he does sometimes—anxiously overlooked by the little pale-haired wife—take this infant, who is so much more concerned for the present by teething than by salvation, on his knee and attempt, if not to derive joy from her, at least to relieve his wife of the nursing.

Certainly he will never drive that child and her mother, however fractious she may be, out of his house. Certainly he will one day love that child with all the force of his charming character.

# IV

## O. B. D.

WHEN a man becomes converted the Salvation Army nurses him carefully until he is strong in the new life; that is to say, experienced officers visit him several times in the day, encourage him in his new purpose, and, above all, deepen in his mind the conviction that someone cares for him.

The conversion of the Puncher, which was so important a matter to the corps in that quarter of London, was watched over by the angel-adjutant. She paid visits to him in his home, dropped in to see him at his work, and waylaid him, with affection, on his way home.

He was at work in a carriage-builder's factory, and the proprietor of the establishment was an infidel. But between this man and the adjutant was one point in common, music; both played the concertina and loved it above all the instruments. "Oh, I only played in an ordinary way," the adjutant tells me; adding with enthusiasm, "but *he* was a master."

It was the concertina which made it possible for the Christian to invade the premises of the infidel. Adjutant and carriage proprietor had many pleasant and quite amiable conversations. In this busy factory in the midst of London, they talked of music, and the angel, watching over the Puncher's conversion, softened the asperities of the infidel's worship of the No-God.

One day she was talking to the Puncher in the carriage factory, when he said to her, "I wish you'd have a talk with the man who comes round here with the papers; he's proper low; they call him Old Born Drunk; and he looks it. But I was almost like that myself, not so very long ago. No one can be hopeless, after me. I wish you'd speak to him." Thus early in his conversion did the Puncher—that quiet and mysterious personality—manifest what one calls his "passion for souls."

The little adjutant waited one day to see this man who had a newspaper round, and who visited the carriage factory to serve the workmen with betting news.

She had seen many of the lowest and most depraved people in London, but until she saw Old Born Drunk never had she realized the hideousness and repulsive abomination to which vice can degrade the human body.

This man, the child of frightfully drunken parents, had been born in drink, and was almost certainly, as his name declared, actually born drunk. He had been taught to drink and had acquired an insatiable appetite for drink in earliest

childhood.  He was now, at the age of five- or
six-and-forty, habitually drunk—sodden.

The vileness of his clothing and the unhealthy
appearance of his flesh did not strike the adjutant
till afterwards.  Her whole attention was held in
a kind of horror by the aspect of the man's eyes.
They were terrible with soullessness.  She racks
her brain in vain to find words to describe them.
She returns again and again to the word *stupefied*.
That is the word that least fails to misrepresent
what no language can describe.  Stupefied!  Not
weakness, not feebleness; not cunning, not depravity; but stupor.  They were the eyes of a
man neither living nor dead; they were the eyes
of nothing that had ever lived or could ever die—
the eyes of eternal stillborn stupor.

These eyes were hardly discernible, for the
flaccid lids hung over the pupils, and the bagged
flesh of the swollen white face pressed upon them
from below.  There was just a disc of glazed
luminosity showing in each dwindled socket—a
disc of veiling existence, perishing life, of stupor.

For the rest he was a true Miserable, lower
than anything to be found among barbarous na-
tions, debased almost out of humanity.  He was
short, thick-set, misshapen, vile; clothed in rags
which suffocated those who blundered near to him
—a creature whom ragged children mocked with
scorn as he passed down the street.

Civilization had produced this man.  He had

his place in London; repulsive as one may find it to contemplate him, he was one of our contemporaries; to the Salvationist he represented a soul.

She said to him, " You don't look very happy. Are you? " He looked, in his dazed fashion, into her clear eyes and kept silence, as though he had lost both the power of speech and the ability to understand it. She said, " Perhaps I could be of some service to you; will you let me try? Will you let me come and see you in your home? "

Old Born Drunk could not speak. She approached quite close to him, bent her kind eyes towards those terrible eyes of stupor, and said, " I want to help you. I know something about your life. They call you Old Born Drunk. Well, Old Born Drunk, let me come and pay you a visit, and make friends with you. There may be many little ways in which I can help you. Let me try."

She made him at last understand. He told her where he lived. Soon afterwards she called upon him.

He occupied a single room, for which he paid seven shillings a week, in a street more notorious for abject destitution than for crime and degradation. She was not in the least afraid of visiting this place, but when she opened the door of the room—good and angelic as she is—the little adjutant almost turned and ran away. Such a smell issued from the den as stifled the lungs and made the spirit heave and shudder with disgust.

Guy de Maupassant has described the odours of a peasant's domicile, with a strength and power of truth which are unforgettable. Something of the same old sour reek, but intensified to loathsomeness by London squalor and slum air, hung like a thick curtain in this den of Old Born Drunk. Guy de Maupassant speaks of the smell of milk, apples, smoke, and that indefinable odour of old houses—smell of the earth, smell of the walls, smell of the furniture, smell of ancient spilled soup, and ancient washings, and old poor peasants; smell of animals and people living together, smell of things and of beings, a smell of Time—the smell of the Past.

In the den of Old Born Drunk there were all these several smells, even the smell of animals, for the place was like a menagerie.

A dog lifted itself up on the vile coverlet of an unmade bed, and growled at the intruder. A litter of guinea-pigs scuttered across the bare and filthy boards of the floor, disappearing under the bed. Rabbit-hutches, with the dusky shapes of their inmates dimly seen behind wire netting, emitted a thick and stifling smell. There were cats on a sack by the hearth. Hanging from the ceiling in front of the closed window was a cage of doves.

This London interior was dark as well as

stifling. A fog seemed to pervade it from dirty wall to dirty wall, from dark ceiling to reeking floor. A figure moved out of this fog, while the dog growled on the unmade bed; it became gradually something that suggested a woman—a creature thin, emaciated, woebegone, clothed almost entirely in sacking. She stood before the Salvationist, in all her wretchedness and squalor; a thing really lower than the animals among whom she spent her life; a woman—the woman who loved Old Born Drunk. Consider the miracle. Imagine to what misery a woman can be brought that she should marry such a man. Reflect that this woman loved him.

The adjutant entered the room and talked to this miracle—the woman who loved Old Born Drunk. The birds and animals provided a topic of conversation. She discovered that they belonged to the child of these two poor people. Yes, they had a child, a new life had been born into this den; and these animals and birds were the boy's pets.

The mother fetched a photograph and handed it to the visitor, not without pride. Astonished, the adjutant beheld in this picture a bright, handsome, and well-dressed boy. The intelligence in his face, and the self-respect in his bearing filled her with amazement. She could hardly believe that he was the child of these parents.

" This is your son? " she asked.

"Yes," said the woman, in her weary way. "He don't look it, do he? But we've been very careful with him, and he's in a good situation, so perhaps he'll be all right. We hope he will, at all events."

Then the adjutant discovered that these frightful parents—in the midst of their destitution and degradation—loved this one child with a self-abnegation and devotion quite wonderful in its purity and strength. For him the den reeked, because when he visited them he liked to see his old pets; and for him those pets had been bought, in the first place, out of coppers earned on the newspaper round, and denied, God knows with what struggle, to a publican by a dipsomaniac, by poor Old Born Drunk, who had this one pure passion growing like a white flower in the corruption of his soul. The drunkard and his wife loved their son. The den was his home.

The Salvationist made this boy the lever of her appeal. She came constantly to the vile den, and saw the parents together. They were both easily convinced of her first premiss, that life would be certainly more comfortable for them if Old Born Drunk signed the pledge and kept it. But even the wife, who was not a drunkard, appeared to agree with her husband that such a consummation lay quite in the realms of fantasy. "You see," said his wife, "he's been used to it from a little 'un; it's meat and drink to him;

look at his name, Old Born Drunk! I really don't think he'd be good for anything if he was to give it up, I don't really." As for Old Born Drunk himself, he did not argue the question; he merely left it with a great silence in the region of the impossible. He listened to the chatter of the women as a philosopher might heed for a moment the notes of quarrelling sparrows.

But the adjutant's kindness and humanity did so far appeal to these two Londoners as to induce them to attend some of the services at the local hall. They left their menagerie, and in their poor vile rags came to the evening meetings, and sat with the Miserables at the back of the hall, listening to the band, listening to the hymns, listening to the praying and preaching, feeling the warmth, brightness, and cleanness of the atmosphere— thinking something in their minds of which we have no knowledge.

Both of them appeared stupefied on these occasions. Apparently the service had no meaning for them. In just such a similar manner two owls in a belfry might listen to church music. They came, they sat, they disappeared.

The adjutant began to feel that they had fallen below the depths to which human sympathy can reach. Her officers used to say, in despair, " They don't seem to understand a word that is said to them." It was this deep stupor of the two Miserables which made for hopelessness and despair. One did not feel their sins or their wretchedness a bar; but this terrible stupor of the understanding was like a thick impenetrable curtain let down between their souls and the light. No one could reach them. They did not understand.

Just about this time the Puncher and the adjutant conceived the idea of a great and stirring revival. The Puncher and those whom he had influenced—it must be carefully remembered that these men were once the terrors of the neighbourhood—agreed that they would make a public exhibition of themselves in the worst streets, and afterwards confess the whole story of their lives, man by man, in the hall. Do not let it be thought that any one of these men contemplated the exhibition with delight. They had to screw their courage to the ordeal; remember, there were their wives to be thought of, as well as a vast mob.

The Puncher—that quiet, pale-faced, sorrowful desirer of souls—inspired the little corps with fortitude. " God has done a lot for us," he said; " we oughtn't to mind doing a bit for Him." The angel-adjutant listened to the ideas of these men, and the revival was planned.

The first effort took the form of a procession through the worst streets of the neighbourhood, at their most crowded hour of the evening, a procession of horse-drawn trolleys, with the converted terrors of the neighbourhood posed in

various attitudes suggesting their past lives—
such, for instance, as a man in convict's dress
suffering the penalty of his crimes.

The streets were thronged. While the trolleys
made their way through the multitude, the adjutant and her assistants passed among the crowd,
inviting people to attend the meeting in the hall.
The result was such a pack as never before had
filled the large meeting-place. Among this vast
audience were Old Born Drunk and his wife,
who had come early on the invitation of the
adjutant.

The meeting began with a hymn, a reading of
the parable of the Prodigal Son, a brief prayer,
and then followed testimonies by the converted
men. One after another they stood up, told how
they had suffered, told how they had sunk to the
gutter, and how their homes were now happy,
their lives clean, and their hearts glad. In the
words of Professor James, these simple men of
the people told their fellows how they had been
consciously wrong, inferior, and unhappy, and
how they were now become, by the mercy of God,
consciously right, superior, and happy.

The angel-adjutant then made her appeal. She
declared that anybody in that hall, never mind
how vile and deserted and shameful, could become
in an instant radiant with happiness and peace,
by coming to the penitent form, kneeling there,
and asking God to forgive him his sins. She

couid point to the men on the platform as living proofs of her assurance.

Several people rose from their seats, most of them with that quiet dogged stolidity of the London workman, characteristic of his whole life, and advanced to the penitent form, like men who had to go through with something distasteful and hard. Some of them said, " God be merciful to me a sinner!" others bowed and were silent; many of the women were crying.

At the back of these penitents came Old Born Drunk and his wife.

The adjutant and her officers were more astonished than all the rest of the people in the meeting. They knew, what the others did not realize, the impenetrable stupefaction of the man's mind, his total obfuscation of soul. For the others, he was only a particularly dirty, particularly vile, particularly drunken one-of-themselves.

The adjutant approached the poor old man as he reached the bench. The small dulled eyes were wet with tears. She put a hand on his arm, and he said to her, in a crying tone, " Oh, I want to be like Joe!"—one of the men who had testified.*

Afterwards he said to her, " While I was listening to Joe, thinking of what he's been, and seeing what he's become, all of a sudden it took me that I'd find God and get Him to make me like Joe.

* His story is told under the title of " The Criminal."

It took me like that.  I just felt, all of a sudden,
*determined* to find God.  *Determined!*" he repeated, with energy astonishing in this broken and
hopeless creature of alcoholism.  " And," he went
on, " while I was kneeling, while I was praying,
I felt the spirit of God come upon me.  I said,
' Oh, God, make me like Joe! ' and while I
prayed, I felt the spirit come upon me.  I *knew*
I could become like Joe.  I know I'm saved."

He was quite emphatic.  But, the adjutant,
knowing the power of temptation, realizing the
saturation of this man's whole being by alcohol,
feared greatly for the stability of his salvation.
She feared chiefly on one account.  The newspaper round by which he earned daily bread in-
cluded practically all the public-houses in that
quarter.  Unless some other work could be found
for Old Born Drunk, surely he must fall some
day, surely the temptation would one day prove
too strong for him.  On the other hand, if work
of a different kind could be found for him, even
this sunken dipsomaniac might, by the grace of
God, make fight against his madness.  It was
just possible.  She had seen miracles almost as
wonderful.

She went to discuss things with Old Born
Drunk.

He sat and listened to all she said with the old
dazed stupor in his eyes, apparently not understanding one of the kind and considerate words

that were said to him. The adjutant turned to his wife, "Is there no other work he can do? Doesn't he feel that he would like some kind of work that he has seen other men doing?"

The wife looked at her husband, "Do you, dear?"

He began to move his lips, considering how to express his thoughts. Then he said, "I don't want anything else." He paused a moment, glancing from the guinea-pigs on the floor to the grimy window. "I must show them," he said, "that I *am* converted."

The adjutant endeavoured to make him realize his danger. For weeks, for months, he might be able to withstand temptation. But, if the moment came, some day in the future, when, perhaps, he was not well, or felt unhappy—might he not fail? She made him, or rather she tried to make him, see that conversion is a long road. The first glow dies away; one sees beyond this lifting glory a long straight road running to life's end. One rises from one's knees to trudge that long road. First, one mounts up with wings, like an eagle; then one runs, and is not weary; finally, the grand climax—one must walk and not faint. The adjutant laboured to bring this conviction home to the understanding of the dipsomaniac.

The man said, "I must show them that I *am* converted."

The adjutant continued to watch over this

brand plucked from the burning. He remained
firm. She asked him if he ever felt tempted.
He replied, " The appetite has gone." They
watched him go in and out of the public-houses—
he was unafraid. The other converts paid him
visits in his den; they all asked the same question,
Did he feel quite sure that drink had no temptation for him? Always the same answer, " The
appetite has gone." It seemed true. And yet,
how inconceivable!

One day he entered a public-house crowded
with workmen. It was Saturday afternoon.
Pockets were full of money. Wives and children were forgotten. The place was a din of
loud voices and coarse laughter. Old Born
Drunk approached the counter with his journals.

There is always a spirit of festivity and good-
humour in a public-house on Saturday after-
noons. The workmen, after a pot or two of beer,
are inclined to horse-play. One of the drinkers
exclaimed, " Hullo, God strike me dead, if this
isn't Old Born Drunk! Come here, daddy; I'll
stand you a pot. We'll wet the Salvation Army."

Old Born Drunk served out his papers. The
workman called for a pot of beer.

" Here, drink, you old ——!" he exclaimed,
forcing the pot towards the convert.

Old Born Drunk shook his head.

" Come, drink it, like a man! What's a pot to
you? Gallons is your mark. Drink it!"

" No."

" Look here, daddy; you're poor, aren't you? "

" Yes."

" Got the missus and the kid to feed? "

" Yes."

" A bob'd make a lot of difference to you, wouldn't it?  See here, daddy; I'll give you a bob, straight, I will—ah, honour bright—if you'll drink this pot.  Smell it.  Smell it, old cock. Ain't it good?  Come along, drink it and earn a bob."

" Not me."

" You won't? "

" No."

" Not for a bob? "

" Not for thousands."

" You mean it? "

" Yes."

" Then have it outside "—and with that the mocking workman flung the whole pot of beer into the old man's face.

There was laughter at this, laughter, too, at the pitiful figure of the old drenched man, blinking his eyes, shaking the drops from his face, wiping the liquor from his mouth and chin.

" Don't it smell good, daddy? " laughed the tormentor.  " 'Ain't beer got a lovely smell to it? You silly old fool!  Why didn't you take it inside, instead of out?  Come here, I'll give you another drop. I'll stand you one. You shan't have the shilling, but you shall have the beer."

"I don't want it," said the old man.

His firmness, his quietness under persecution, moved the rough men in the bar. One of them "took up a subscription." Old Born Drunk left the place with a pocket full of money. Also, he left it as a hero.

Weeks, months, years passed away. The old fellow remained firm. And he made little economies, in spite of subscriptions to the local corps of the Salvation Army. One day he was rich enough to take a tiny shop in the neighbourhood. His wife and son moved out of the dreadful den, and began a new life, full of happiness. They entered the ranks of respectability.

It was the old fellow's steadfastness and lasting fortitude which made both his wife and the son join the Salvation Army. This represented the height of earthly happiness to Old Born Drunk, because he had all along nursed one great hope in the profound of his being—the hope that some day his son would be an officer in the Army, that is to say, would devote all his life to the work. Old Born Drunk was not fit for such high work; it was necessary for him to earn his living; all he could do was to attend the meetings, march behind the band, saying a word or two in private to those of his customers who were sad and unhappy. But his son had book learning, his son was good—he might perhaps be one day an officer in this great, merciful, and universal army of salvation.

This once ruined creature was now happy and whole. His conversion appeared so extraordinary to the people in the neighbourhood, extraordinary in its lastingness as well as in its effects, that he became a power for righteousness without exerting any missionary zeal. People looked at him in the streets. Vicious and degraded men at street corners, or at the doors of public-houses, regarded the old man, born again and living in respectability and happiness, with something of the same stirring in their brains as once had made him exclaim, " I want to be like Joe." He advertised salvation.

Religion to these people is not a theology. It is a fact. They are not mystical. They are incapable of definitions. Old Born Drunk himself could not have told you anything about the articles of his religion or his conception of the nature of God. He only knew that God had saved him, directly he sought salvation with a determined mind. He only knew that instantly he had been delivered from absolute wretchedness. He only knew that he was now very happy.

And this is also what the outcasts saw in him. They saw that perhaps the very lowest man in the whole neighbourhood, the man, at any rate, most sunken in drunkenness, was now walking in their midst, clean, happy, and respectable. He had got religion. Religion had done the miracle. Religion was a good thing, if only a man could once make up his mind to take the step. Look at Old Born Drunk. What a difference religion had made to him! Before the miracle of Old Born Drunk the arguments of tavern atheists melted into thin air. Facts are stubborn things, and never more stubborn than when they walk the street and breathe human air.

In this way Old Born Drunk made a profound impression in that quarter of the town. Not, of course, such a marvellous and staggering impression as that produced by the Puncher's conversion, but a quiet and very lasting impression. He was discussed in that locality, as a novel or a picture in another quarter of the town. Never a public-house argument about religion that did not end with, " Well, anyhow, what about Old Born Drunk?"

One day the adjutant learned that he was ill. She went at once to see him. He was dying.

She sat at his bedside very often while he was waiting for death, and he talked to her then, not more fluently than he had talked heretofore, but with more candour.

She said to him once, " Well, you have fought the good fight, dear old friend. You never looked back. You never fell. It has been a great victory. It has blessed others besides yourself. I

can tell you now that many thought you would
not be able to last. They thought that the appetite would return, and that it would prove too
strong for you. Many, many people have prayed
that you might have strength in that moment, if
it ever came."

He smiled wistfully, and said to her, " You used
to think as how it was the drink that might come
upon me again. It wasn't that. God took all
desire for it clean away from me. No; that
wasn't the miracle. The greatest miracle was—
the pipe!"

Then he told her that all through those years,
when they thought the temptation to drink was
tearing his soul, he was putting up a tremendous
fight with the one appetite that would not leave
him, the appetite for tobacco.

His struggle had been secret to himself. It
had been almost intolerable. At times he felt that
he must go mad. There was something in his
brain which was like a devil, urging him with the
most pitiless and unceasing force to the nulling
narcotic of nicotine. Always. Never had it left
him. And he had fought it, not because he felt
that it was sinful to smoke, not even that he
feared it might re-create his appetite for drink,
but because he wanted to be as good a soldier
as he could, to give up everything for God.

And so, on his dying bed, this old Londoner,
picked from the gutter and restored to humanity,

contemplated as the great miracle, not his conversion, not his total and mysterious freedom from alcoholism, but the ability with which God had provided him to withstand the passion for his pipe.  Always the torture had been present, always strength had been sufficient to withstand it.

Just before the moment of his death, the adjutant said to him, " You are quite happy?  You know that God has forgiven you everything? "

He answered, " I am without fear."

In that neighbourhood people still talk about Old Born Drunk, and they like to impress those who will listen with the wonder of his funeral. He was given what is called " an Army funeral," that is to say, he was buried with the military honours of salvation, just as a great soldier, a national hero, is buried with martial pomp. Thousands of people lined the streets and followed the procession to the cemetery.  The entire district turned out like one man to see the last of Old Born Drunk—to stare, perhaps, at the pageant, to be influenced, however, whether they wished it or not, by the good end of a brave fighter.  A stranger entering that quarter of the town would have thought that the populace had turned out for the funeral of their prince.

Such is the extraordinary parochialism of London, a truth of the metropolis little realized by the casual observer.  A few hundred yards away from that particular quarter of the town, no one had heard of Old Born Drunk. In that particular quarter he was more famous, more watched, more discussed than the greatest heroes of the nation.

His death was an event. His salvation was a profound impression. The quarter of the town in which he lived and died feels to this day, and will feel through many generations, the effect of his salvation.

# V

## THE CRIMINAL

A GREAT step will be taken towards the abolition of crime when the State recognizes that criminals are human beings extremely like ourselves. It is quite a fair thing to say of the mass of civilized mankind that their primary objective in existence is money; and it is no less fair to say that the vast majority desire to get more money than is necessary for their actual needs with as little labour as possible. Indeed, the whole spirit of modern politics and trade organizations, in its ultimate purpose, represents this individual search after as large a reward as possible for as little exertion as may be. Higher wages and shorter hours of employment is the respectable and social formula of that disreputable and anti-social energy which actuates the criminal mind, and expresses itself in the familiar formulæ of thieves' philosophy.*

But there is something else. The criminal is

---

* Mr. Havelock Ellis quotes in his book a few inscriptions made by convicts on the walls of their cells. Such as: "The Lord says it is good to be here." "Cheer up, girls, it's no use to fret." The philosophy of the criminal is to bear punishment, and take care not to be caught next time.

often heroic in his character, superior to the ruck, a man of daring, romance, and adventure.

Mr. Havelock Ellis quotes endless authorities in his book on *The Criminal* to prove that those whom we call enemies of society are only following impulses which were praiseworthy in another age, and which are even in this age practised by a great many people who flourish in the front ranks of our industrial civilization. " Of a very great number of modern habitual criminals," says one authority, " it may be said that they have the misfortune to live in an age in which their merits are not appreciated. Had they been in the world a sufficient number of generations ago, the strongest of them might have been chiefs of a tribe. . . . With the disposition and the habits of uncivilized men which he has inherited from a remote past, the criminal has to live in a country where the majority of the inhabitants have learned new lessons of life, and where he is regarded more and more as an outcast as he strives more and more to fulfil the yearnings of his nature."

Another authority says, " Some of them at least would have been the ornament and the moral aristocracy of a tribe of Red Indians." Another, " The criminal of to-day is the hero of our old legends. We put in prison to-day the man who would have been the dreaded and respected chief of a clan or tribe." Another exclaims, " How many of Homer's heroes would to-day be in a

convict prison, or, at all events, despised as violent
and unjust? "

We may also see with but very little effort of
observation that there are a great many public
men enjoying the reward of fortune at the present day whose success in financial jugglery has
been won by methods exactly similar to the criminal's more blundering attempts after the wealth
of other people. Every time a company-pro-
moting case occurs in the law courts, although by
his knowledge of the company-law and the difficulty of obtaining evidence in such cases, the de-
fendant may escape prison, every man of affairs
knows that he is a blackguard of the lowest kind,
a criminal set upon getting other people's money
by dishonest means, and a rogue as greatly de-
serving penal servitude as any burglar or petty
larcener in a convict prison.

As to when criminal instincts first manifest
themselves, one who had visited juvenile offend-
ers in Tothill Fields wrote: " On our return
. . . we consulted with some of our friends
as to the various peccadilloes of their youth, and
though each we asked had grown to be a man of
some little mark in the world, both for intellect
and honour, they, one and all, confessed to having
committed in their younger days many of the very
' crimes ' for which the boys at Tothill Fields are
incarcerated. For ourselves, we will frankly confess, that at Westminster School, where we passed

some seven years of our boyhood, such acts were daily perpetrated; and yet if the scholars had been sent to the House of Correction, instead of Oxford or Cambridge, to complete their education, the country would now have seen many of our playmates working among the convicts in the Dockyards, rather than lending dignity to the senate or honour to the bench."

The story which I am about to tell in this place is the narrative of a modern criminal which emphasizes everything that has ever been written on the subject by anthropologists and criminologists; but, as the end will prove, it shows that even in a mind penetrated and interpenetrated with anti-social instincts there is some one thing to which appeal may be made, and by which such reform can be effected as to lead to a complete spiritual regeneration. Psychology cannot neglect this regenerating influence and call itself a complete science of the human mind. Criminologists and prison reformers can effect little for the permanent improvement of the habitual criminal without the employment of this force. One power, and one alone, can make the habitual criminal a good man in the loftiest and only lasting sense of that term, and that force is religion.

Born in the slums of London, with parents rather better than the average, the man in this story, whom we will call Joe, found himself with the streets for his only playground, and with bad boys for the only companions worthy of his friendship. He was so enormously strong, so full of daring, so conscious of restriction and limitation in the narrowness of his circumstance, that he must needs fling himself heart and soul into the dare-devil adventures of boys hungry for a big life and bold enough to fight for it.

No Sunday-school could hold such a boy; no second-hand religion in a respectable church could impress his mind with the reality of spiritual things. He found himself surrounded by bricks and walls, and he wanted adventure. He felt himself capable of doing things worthy of a novelette, and he saw a policeman at the street corner. It became evident to him that if he wanted to fulfil the passion of his body, he must dare the police and find his adventures in the streets. To every powerful impulse of his nature society had set up circumambient opposition. It was necessary to make war upon society.

He was in prison at nine years of age.

Before getting into prison he had encountered the social law. He had stolen more clumsily than was his wont a piece of meat, with the result that he got eight strokes with the birch-rod. This punishment did not check him. He aimed at higher game. To be a petty thief did not satisfy his buccaneering ambitions. He conceived the idea of a burglary. The respectable reader, shocked by the thought of a child of nine com-

mitting burglary, must ask himself whether at
that age he was not stealing sugar from the side-
board cupboard or candied-peel from the larder.
He must remember, too, that this child of nine
had been marched triumphantly to a police-court,
had had the honour of appearing before a magistrate, and had been hardened by a birching. If,
after this experience, he had played the lamb,
what would the young lions of the slums have
thought about him? Be it remembered that this
boy was lion-hearted, bold, daring, brave, strong,
and indifferent to punishment.

I tried to discover what had worked in his mind
at this time, and he could only tell me that he
wanted to be daring, wanted to feel himself big.
The meek children of that neighbourhood went
to Sunday-school; he regarded them with contempt; a certain section were neither good nor
bad, neither respectable nor disreputable, they
did not interest him, did not satisfy him; others,
the very elect, brave, bold, dauntless, and tre-
mendously masculine, roused in his mind the
greatest force in childhood—admiration. He
wanted to be like these fine fellows. He not only
wanted to feel that he was clever at stealing, but
also that he feared nothing, neither policeman,
judge, prison, nor hangman's rope—like these
bloods of the slum.

It is necessary to know something of a boy's
life in the slums—its conditions, its dullness, its

surrounding influences, and its limitations—to understand the swift growth and vigorous development of criminality in the minds of quite young children.

Boys of a strong animal temperament—whose innocence has long departed, and who inhabit often enough the same bedroom as their fathers and mothers—find themselves in streets full of shops and barrows where there is a profusion of everything the body can desire, even a profusion of things coveted by low and sensual minds—such as the barrow of vicious photographs, the empty shop employed as a penny-gaff for exhibiting the nude, and those miserable penny-in-the-slot machines whose pictures are so vile and so vulgar. To enjoy these things money is necessary, and the only romantic way of getting money is by stealing; the only way of getting food and tobacco and pictures without money is by stealing them.

The homes from which these boys come into the streets, where so much wealth is displayed, are bad enough as sleeping-places, but as living-rooms they are quite horrible. To a high-spirited boy conscious of desire for a full-blooded life of adventure they are impossible. He must have movement, the excitement of danger, the enjoyment of forbidden pleasures.

" Have you ever realized," Mr. Thomas Holmes once asked me, " what it is to live below the poverty line? Not in the family of the well-to-do mechanic, with his club and his union; but right down—down in the kennels and cellars and gutters? Think what your manhood would have been if your childhood had passed in a garret, where your mother made matchboxes for fourteen hours a day, and at the end of the week earned nine shillings. In that room you would have eaten your meals—save the mark!—toiled over the paste-pot before you went to school and after you came from school, and then you would have crawled into a corner to sleep on a mattress with the rest of the family. That dingy world would have been your world, your environment." *

Then there is this most important factor to bear in mind—the vanity of the daring child, the swagger of the masculine boy which becomes so easily the well-known vanity of the criminal. Hear Mr. Havelock Ellis on this head:

" The vanity of criminals is at once an intellectual and an emotional fact. It witnesses at once to their false estimate of life and of themselves, and to their egotistic delight in admiration. They share this character with a large proportion of artists and literary men, though, as Lombroso remarks, they decidedly excel them in this respect. The vanity of the artist and literary man marks the abnormal element, the tendency in them to

* *Master Workers.*

degeneration.    It reveals in them the weak points
of a mental organization, which at other points
is highly developed.    Vanity may exist in the
well-developed ordinary man, but it is unobtru-
sive; in its extreme forms it marks the abnormal
man, the man of unbalanced mental organization,
artist or criminal.

" George Borrow, who was so keen a student
of men, has some remarks on the vanity of criminals in regard to dress: ' There is not a set of
people in the world more vain than robbers in
general, more fond of cutting a figure whenever
they have an opportunity, and of attracting the
eyes of their fellow-creatures by the gallantry of
their appearance.    The famous Sheppard of olden
times delighted in sporting a suit of Genoese
velvet, and when he appeared in public generally
wore a silver-hilted sword at his side; whilst
Vaux and Hayward, heroes of a later day, were
the best-dressed men on the *pavé* of London.
Many of the Italian bandits go splendidly deco-
rated, and the very gypsy robber has a feeling
for the charms of dress; the cap alone of the
Haram Pasha, the leader of the cannibal gypsy
band which infested Hungary towards the conclusion of the century, was adorned with gold and
jewels of the value of four thousand guilders.
Observe, ye vain and frivolous, how vanity and
crime harmonize.    The Spanish robbers are as
fond of this species of display as their brethren

of other lands, and, whether in prison or out of it, are never so happy as when, decked out in a profusion of white linen, they can loll in the sun, or walk jauntily up and down.' " He then describes the principal features of Spanish robber foppery.

" More significant and even more widely spread is the moral vanity of criminals. ' In ordinary society,' said Vidocq, ' infamy is dreaded; among a body of prisoners the only shame is not to be infamous; to be an *escarpe* (assassin) is the highest praise.' This is universally true among every group of murderers or of thieves, the author of a large criminal transaction is regarded by all his fellows as a hero, and he looks down upon the others with contempt; the man who has had the misfortune to be imprisoned for a small or, in the opinion of criminal society, disreputable offence, represents himself as the author of some crime of magnitude.

" A Russian youth of nineteen killed an entire family. When he heard that all St. Petersburg was talking of him, he said, ' Now my schoolfellows will see how unfair it was of them to say that I should never be heard of.' " *

The Abbé Moreau, describing the arrival of a great criminal at the prison of La Grande Roquette, says that he is immediately surrounded, though the curiosity remains respectful, and is

* *The Criminal,* by Havelock Ellis.

a king in the midst of his subjects; " envious looks are cast at those privileged individuals who have succeeded in placing themselves near him; they listen eagerly for his slightest word; they do not speak their admiration for fear of interrupting him, and he knows that he dominates and fascinates them."

Essential to a true understanding of the young criminal is the full apprehension of that immense respect with which great crime inspires the daring members of society whose blood clamours for adventure, whose bodies are insufficiently nourished, and whose minds are insufficiently subjected to discipline.

When Joe came back to his mates from that first birching he was very little wickeder than the average schoolboy; but mark the swift growth of the criminal.

His vanity to appear a fine fellow in the eyes of his rough mates led him not only to make light of his disgrace and its sufferings, but to propose things a great deal more daring and dangerous. He wanted to be a burglar before he was ten years of age.

Before he committed burglary, in the technical sense of that term, he shone as a hero among his fellows in other forms of crime requiring swiftness of execution and no little daring. It was one of his favourite tricks to enter a shop which he had reconnoitred with the cunning of a Red

Indian, and to vault the counter, fill both hands from the till, and make his escape before the shopkeeper had risen from his chair in the back parlour. Another of his ways of getting money was to obtain goods at various shops in his mother's name, and to sell them at half-price to other people. He made a habit of playing high-wayman to boys sent on errands by their mothers, forcing those poor frightened children to deliver up either their money or their packages.

To return tamely home after some of these escapades not only was dangerous but dreadfully uninteresting. He became one of a gang who slept out—slept either in common lodging-houses or in the open streets. He was not in the least ashamed when a policeman laid him by the heels and he went to prison.

It was at the age of fourteen that he committed his first technical burglary.

There was a jeweller's shop in the neighbour-hood which exhibited a tempting show of silver-plate in its windows. This shop occupied a corner, and a garden wall alone separated Joe from its back premises. To climb that wall at night, to enter the house, and to get away with some of the silver-plate, seemed to him a perfectly easy and quite a delightful adventure. He worked it all out with some of his mates, and dreamed great dreams of glory till the night came round for the crime.

Everything favoured these wild boys—a dark night, empty streets, an absence of police. Joe climbed the wall, disappeared on the other side, and his mates waited in the street to receive the plunder when he returned. As though born to the job of housebreaking, Joe found it easy to force a window, to raise the sash without making a noise, to enter the premises, and find his way in the dark to the shop and the silver. He made his haul—listened to hear if anyone was stirring —and then stole out through the window, crossed the garden, and climbed the wall. All was perfectly still and silent. He saw figures in the darkness beneath him, descended into their midst, and found himself held by four policemen.

He was not then fourteen years of age, and the law sentenced him to fifteen months' imprisonment.

The birching was a light matter, but fifteen months of prison fare, prison solitude, and prison discipline, this was terrible to the boy. He did not feel any horror of himself, any fear of hell, any desire for goodness, but in his prison cell this London boy determined that he would give up his mates, mend his ways, and live a life in which the police could never interfere. He tells me he suffered terrible remorse, and used to cry in his cell; but when I question him it is to discover that he felt only the inconvenience of prison, the wretchedness of his fare, and the horrible, maddening deprivation of his liberty. A boy who has ever endured three hours' "detention" on a half-holiday may guess what this strong-limbed, daring lad of fourteen suffered during those dragging fifteen months of prison.

But when he came out, there was nothing in his heart except bitterness and rage. Far from mending him, far from creating in him any desire for goodness, uprightness, and a life of useful work, prison had only made the lad a deadly hater of law, and a sworn enemy of society. He determined to plot against society and to beat it at its own game.

Within three months of his release he was arrested and sent to a truant school. This punishment also failed to reform his character. He came out from it to receive in quick succession nine sentences, each of a month, for thefts of various kinds.

He was now marked down as incorrigible, ticketed by the police as one of the criminal classes. People pointed at him in the streets, policemen gave him a look as he went by, sometimes followed him.

He now began to work as a real burglar, associating with notorious cracksmen. He heard in one of the public-houses he frequented of a man, the owner of a laundry, who kept all his money in the breast pocket of his overcoat, which he always hung at night on the peg of his bedroom door. Sometimes, it was said, that pocket contained as much as fifteen or twenty pounds.

Joe studied the house, made himself acquainted with its plan, and one night set out to pick the pocket of that overcoat hanging from the bedroom door. His account of this crime made one feel something of the terror associated with desperate burglars. He is a man above the medium height, of a thin and wasted frame, but with broad shoulders and a large greyish face; the forehead low, the head round, the eyes big, searching, menacing; the voice full of a quick decision and a certain hard brutality.

"I slipped out one night from a public-house," he told me, "walked into dark streets until I had dodged all the police that were watching me, and then made my way to the laundryman's house. There was a wall that a cat could climb easier than I could, but I nipped over it, and lay in the garden, listening to hear if I had disturbed anybody. Not a sound. I went to the back of the house, found a window that was all right, opened it with only a creak or two, waited on the sill for five or ten minutes to hear if anybody was stirring, and then stepped quietly inside. Quietly! I went bang into a bath of water, stumbled, fell, and made such a clatter that I woke the people up. I heard the wife say, 'There's someone downstairs!' And I heard the man say, 'Go along with you; it's only a cat.' The wife persisted. The husband told her to shut up. I stood where I was in the dark bath-house for a solid hour. Then I moved, groping my way. I found the hall, crept to the stairs, and listened. Nothing could be heard, except a clock ticking. I waited, and then went softly up the stairs. When I reached the landing I could hear the man and woman snoring—like a couple of pigs! I remember I felt disgusted by the noise they made. Lor', I never heard anything like it—upon my word, it was just like a couple of pigs. I stood listening to them at that bedroom door—less than an inch of wood between me and the overcoat—for another hour. Then I put my fingers round the handle, turned it very gently, and opened the door. The snoring sounded much louder. There was no light in the room. I hadn't disturbed them in the least. I waited for a few minutes, then slipped my free hand round the door, felt for the overcoat, found the bag of cash, drew it out, slipped it in my pocket, and shut the door as quietly as I had opened it, waited a few minutes to be certain I hadn't disturbed them, and then very slowly went down the stairs. I gave the bath a wide berth, got out of the window, and made off.

" There was twenty-one pounds in the bag, and I went large. I bought myself a new suit of clothes, gave the money to a pal to keep for me, and kept just enough for drinks and cigars till the affair should blow over. But four days afterwards a policeman came to me. ' Joe,' he said, ' where did you get that suit of clothes from? ' ' My cousin gave it to me,' I answered. Not a bit of use. They had me, and I got a stretch."

A few days after he came out he was standing one day looking into a jeweller's shop, when a policeman gripped his arm suddenly from behind and marched him off to the station. In his pocket were found some housebreaking tools. He was sent to prison.

All that he suffered in these imprisonments, so far as his inarticulate subconsciousness can express itself, appears to have been a remorse of the stomach. Every Sunday, half-starved, forsaken, and silent in his prison cell, he reflected on his brothers at the family dinner-table in his father's house. They were not only at liberty; they were enjoying a Sunday dinner. His imagination brought into his cell the rich odours of beef gravy, the flavour of baked potatoes, the taste of white bread, the pleasant smell of hot roast beef fresh and sputtering from the fire. He tells me that he was not maddened by this memory, but saddened to tears. He used to cry softly to himself, swallowing great lumps in his throat, and thinking of all that he missed by being in prison. There are many tears shed in gaols; these places indeed are houses of weeping, and tears for a Sunday dinner are not perhaps in the sight of the spirits vastly different from tears of a more religious contrition. When this man wept for roast beef and fried potatoes, he wept for his past life, just as Verlaine, with a greater gift of expression, wept in the cells of his French prison:

> Le ciel est, par-dessus le toit,
>     Si bleu, si calme!
> Un arbre, par-dessus le toit,
>     Berce sa palme.
>
> La cloche dans le ciel qu'on voit
>     Doucement tinte.
> Un oiseau sur l'arbre qu'on voit
>     Chante sa plainte.
>
> Mon Dieu, mon Dieu, la vie est là,
>     Simple et tranquille.
> Cette paisible rumeur-là
>     Vient de la ville.
>
> —Qu'as-tu fait, o toi que voilà,
>     Pleurant sans cesse,
> Dis, qu'as-tu fait, toi que voilà,
>     De ta jeunesse?

Weeping almost without ceasing, and thinking of his brothers in their father's house, the London burglar, like the Parisian poet, was really weeping for his wasted youth. He got so far in his remorse as to pray, and so real was his bitterness— even if inspired by a Sunday dinner—that his prayers were always for death. He wanted to get out of a world which seemed to have no use for him, a world whose affairs appeared to be governed by policemen who had a " down " on him.   All through his imprisonment he had these fits of remorse, and prayed to die.

Never once—and in this all the prisoners I have ever talked to bear him out—never once did a prison chaplain visit his cell, make an appeal to his higher nature, or show that interest in his life, whether he swam or sank, which an expert like General Booth tells us is the very first step towards the reclamation of the outcast.   I asked him his opinion of the Church services, and he said that they were regarded as opportunities for conversation, that the words of the prayers sounded like a mockery, that singing hymns was pleasant and popular, that the sermons were unintelligible.   In the interviews which a prisoner is supposed to have with the chaplain before release, he was addressed always in the same words (others bear him out in this, too), " Well, I suppose I shall see you back here in a month or two? "   Once he turned round on the chaplain and said, " Yes, and it won't be your fault if you see me back here all my life."   He was conscious that the chaplain ought to have been able to help him.   A strange conviction in the mind of such a man.

We have now to relate something concerning the police which we must preface with a caution to the reader.   It is not intended here to argue that the treatment experienced by Joe, and some others, is in the least typical of the London police.

Many of these men help old prisoners, and are kind to them in divers ways. But this is truth— let a man inspire two or three of the police in his neighbourhood with hate, and that man may be marked down for ceaseless persecution and most cruel tyranny. Whenever men of the class of policemen get a " down " on a man—as for instance, rough-riding corporals in a cavalry regiment on some unfortunate recruit—they sometimes use their power, and exert their authority to make that man's life a hell—in their own phrase, to break him. I do not say in the case of the police that they have not some excuse for this conduct—they are brave men exposed to most cowardly and brutal assaults—but their vengeance is certainly a danger and a great expense to the State. I fear that this private execution of vengeance still goes on; I am sure that the criminal class is made worse by it; I am convinced that the heads of police are unaware of it; moreover, I feel that the police who do these things consider themselves justified in their action, and believe that in executing private vengeance they are furthering the cause of law and order quite as much as getting even with their oppressors. One is not by any means making a general attack upon the London police.

When Joe came out from prison he went, with the money he had earned by prison labour, and asked his father to come for a drink. The old man refused. Joe went to the tavern, bought himself a drink, purchased a little gin for his mother and a few cigars for his father, and returned home with these peace-offerings. Half an hour afterwards he was taking the air, and enjoying the sweets of liberty.

A policeman crossed the road and stopped him. " Joe," he said, in a kindly voice, " an old gentleman has had his watch pinched; the description given answers to you; the inspector thinks you can clear yourself all right, but wants you to step up to the station and give an account of your movements."

" Why, I've only just come out ! " said Joe.

" I know; but the description answers."

Joe walked easily and cheerfully beside the policeman, laughing at those who turned and stared, thinking that Joe was caught again. As he entered the station the policeman suddenly gripped his arm, and ran him before the inspector. " I charge this man," he said, " with drunkenness and begging."

When he was in the cell two or three constables entered. Joe had not handled the police force gently in the past, and he had experienced before police retribution in the station cell. But now he was innocent.

The policemen set about him with their fists and feet, and did not leave him until he was bleeding, bruised, and almost unconscious.

I asked him why he did not hit back, or insist upon seeing the inspector. His answer chimed exactly with the comment of another old gaol-bird who was present, " What would have been the use? " They both smiled at my innocence in asking such a question.

Then these two men told me of how on many occasions they had been the victims of police " justice," of how on many occasions the door of the station cell had opened, and two, three, and four men had entered to pound them unmercifully,—many occasions. Those nights in the cell of the police-station are dreaded by the marked man as much as any part of the prison treatment, except " solitary." The utter uselessness of complaint, the necessity of taking the punishment " lying down," the feeling of its injustice which stirs in their blood—this makes them bitter against the police, and there is no bitterness in the world like an old convict's for the force of law and order.

When Joe came out from imprisonment which followed upon this shameful arrest, he was a man with but one thought in his soul—murder. As he " came down the street " he encountered the policeman who had put him away. The man laughed, and said, " I did you nicely, Joe, didn't I? Cheer up! I'll have you again before long."

" Not without cause, you ——! " said Joe, and walked on.

He waited till dark, and then went to a street with iron railings in front of the areas. A blow with his knee broke a railing in the middle; a wrench with his strong hands at the spike, and he had drawn it out from the cross-bar. This weapon he slipped inside his trousers, and went to meet the constable who had put him away.

The man came along; Joe hid in a doorway. The man drew level with Joe. Out came the iron bar, and with one smashing blow, as the constable passed, one blow which broke the helmet to pieces and cracked the man's skull like an egg-shell, Joe's enemy lay senseless on the pavement.

For this crime he received a long stretch at Dartmoor.

He told me that he has never suffered so much in his life as he suffered during solitary confinement. He said that no words can express the torture of that punishment. A flogging is bad, very bad, but it is not to be compared with the maddening horror of solitary confinement. A diet of bread and water wastes the body to the point of extremest weakness; and in this pitiable condition of physical collapse the mind has to endure solitude, silence, semi-darkness. One day of this punishment is hard to support, but two, three, four—the hardest brute in the world is reduced to whining for mercy.

I asked him what a man does in solitary confinement, and never, so long as I live, shall I forget his answer. It was an answer given not in words, but in a posture. He sat forward on the edge of his chair, rested an elbow on his right knee, placed his fingers against his cheek, and stared at nothingness.

" It's like that all the time," said another gaol-bird, who was present, studying Joe's attitude with a critical and approving glance; " and some-times it's like this." He let his body lean for-ward, set both elbows on his knees, and with his hands on either side of his face, the fingers almost meeting over the head, stared down at the floor.

Joe said to me, " All day long like that—on bread and water. No light, no air, no sound of a voice, no sound of a step, nothing! I reckon a man would rather be hanged than go through solitary."

This man, whose story will disclose a nature very far from indifferent to kindness and sym-pathy, whose brain is acute, observing, and re-flective, and whose whole life is now given to saving the criminal classes, assures me that every fresh imprisonment only hardened him, and de-clares that no one who has really studied prisons, with a knowledge of prisoners, can believe that imprisonment has any other effect than this terri-ble, cruel, and costly effect of hardening and making worse.

He speaks with authority. This man who is grey and looks so old is four-and-thirty. Out of his thirty-four years of life, seventeen have been spent in prison.

This seems a suitable place to quote Thomas Holmes on our prison system: " It is the most senseless, brutal, and wicked of all human schemes for checking crime. Appallingly stupid. When I think of men I know sitting in their dark cells at night—they put them to bed at eight o'clock!— I can almost cry with the pain of it. If the idea is simply to punish, the present system is admirable; it is so supremely devilish. But, I take it, the State, when it gets hold of a man who has broken one of its laws, desires to send him back to the world as speedily as possible, to work honestly and truly for the nation. But what does the prison do? It crucifies the man, and hardens him past redemption. It intensifies his bitterness against society, and adds a horrible darkness to the chaos of his moral nature. Do you know these words of a prisoner?—they are worth remembering: ' I know how many nails there are in the floor within reach of my eye, and the number of the seams also; I am familiar with the stained spots, the splintered furrows, the scratches, and the uneven surface of the planks. The floor is a well-known map to me—the map of monotony —and I con its queer geography all day and at night in dreary dreams. I know the blotches on the whitened wall as well as I know the warts and moles on the hopeless faces opposite me.

My mind is a mill that grinds nothing. Give me work—work for heart and mind—or my heart will lose its last spark of hope, and my brain its last remnant of reason.'

"Think of those words for a night or two, as you move freely about the rooms of your home. And think of them when you wake to an open window and the freshness of a new morning. Think of them. And there are thousands of men penned in like this—whose minds are a mill that grind nothing—every day in a Christian year. It is not sentimental rubbish; it isn't hysterical. Because, don't you see, a criminal is a human being, and in many instances of a most amazingly complex and bewildering fashion."

Sir Oliver Lodge, who is interested in this question of prisons, and has made some study of it, asks, "Are we satisfied with our treatment of criminals? Are we, as a civilized people, content to grow a perennial class of habitual criminals, and to keep them in check only by devices appropriate to savages: hunting them, flogging them, locking them up, and exterminating them?"

At Dartmoor, Joe found something which mitigated the horrors of his existence. In prison there is rather more thieving, I am told, than outside. Every convict is on the look out for "pinching" something; it breaks the monotony merely to look out for the chance of stealing, just as a fisherman will cheerfully go all day

without getting a bite.   But seldom is the convict's look out unrewarded.   He can steal in the
kitchen, in the shops, in the cells.   Also he can
trade with warders, many of whom (the great
majority, I am told), either out of goodness
of heart or to add to their wages, smuggle in
food and plug tobacco for the convicts.   All
this, as I say, breaks the monotony of prison
routine.

One day, as he was working in the corridors of
the prison, Joe saw a handkerchief in one of the
cells.   He " pinched " it.   Some little time afterwards that handkerchief came in useful.   He was
digging with a gang of convicts on the bogs when
he caught sight of two little mice, huddling away
to escape detection.   Swift as thought—I have
never seen man move his hands quicker than
Joe—he bagged the mice; wrapped them in his
handkerchief, and stuffed the booty under the
back of his shirt.   He got back to his cell with
his find undetected.

For sixteen months they delighted the life of
this habitual criminal—those two little mice.   In
the loneliness of his cell he tamed them, taught
them tricks, made them fond of him.   For their
sakes he stole from the kitchen and saved crumbs
from his own meals.   Their sleeping-place was a
bag hanging from the wall of his cell.   In this
bag they produced a family, soon necessitating
greater thefts from the kitchen, and the entire

family was removed from prison when Joe got his liberty and taken back to his father.

Some of the prisoners tame starlings, crows, and sparrows.

One other means Joe discovered to alleviate the dullness of his lot. He instituted a telephone service with the next cell. By the removal of one brick, easily replaced, prisoners can speak to each other in whispers. What they find to talk about can be imagined. It is the gossip of the prison— the cruelty of one warder, the kindness of another, the funk of a third, the theft of this convict, the mutiny of that, and what each man means to do when he gets out.

Joe came out of his sentence more hardened than ever, but more or less out of love with the life that had got him there. He found someone waiting to meet him. It was the converted Puncher.

The Puncher had set himself upon the conversion of this man, the chief terror of the neighbourhood. When drink had brought him down to common lodging-houses, the Puncher had made acquaintance with the Criminal. Both men were big in their own way. The Puncher was a great fighter; the Criminal was a great burglar. The Puncher treated the Criminal as an equal. They drank together, plotted certain villainies together, and in a way consorted. But there was always something which kept them separate. Joe respected the Puncher as a fighting-man, but he thought nothing of him as a criminal. Joe, it must be remembered, had risen so high in his profession of burglar as to work with men like Milsom and Fowler, who thought no little of his cunning, and had the highest respect for his courage. A sentence of twelve months mercifully, for Joe, broke up this partnership just before the famous murder. Another of the men he worked with was high in his profession—Dick Coombs, now serving a life sentence for the murder of his mistress. And another was a notorious criminal with the romantic name of Brighton Slasher, who is now serving his third term of seven years, to say nothing of other terms.

Joe was a first-class burglar, and a man trusted and respected by the best brains in his profession. The Puncher did not, therefore, stoop when he associated with Joe in common lodging-houses, and Joe was not without reason when he held himself at a certain distance from this prize-fighter, fallen into mere drunkenness and stupid violence.

It was of Joe the Puncher thought most longingly after his own conversion. He knew how the wild spirits in that neighbourhood respected Joe. He knew that Joe was looked upon as the most dangerous man in the place. If only this king of the local terrors could be caught, could be made to fling off evil, and stand up clean and straight for right living, what an effect it would produce, what a glory for religion!

So the Puncher waited for Joe, and the two men talked together—Joe hearing what the Puncher had to say, and leaving him with the promise to think it over.

What the Puncher said was merely to point out the discomforts of evil and the comforts of goodness. He asked Joe to compare prison life with freedom, the lodging-house with home, crime with human affection. He could say, " Look at me now, and remember what I was once."

Joe could certainly see a great difference.

But Joe was in the net of crime. His companions came about him. It was quite impossible to escape from them. Soon he was living in the lodging-houses of this dreadful quarter of the town.

One pays fivepence a night in the houses frequented by Joe. You get for this money a single bed in a room containing six; lights are turned out at half-past twelve; and you must leave your bed before nine o'clock in the morning. If you have the " clods " for the next night's doss, you can stay in the kitchen all day. These kitchens can be seen through the street railings; the doors are kicked to pieces, the windows have gone, the interior is lighted chiefly by the fire. Here hangs a general frying-pan beside the fireplace, always dirty. You take your food, cook it, hang the frying-pan up, still dirty, and then eat either on a backless bench or at a filthy table, often surrounded by the lowest creatures in London. This is the general kitchen, and it is here that the police come when they want a particular criminal.

Joe discovered that this environment was too strong for him. He remembered what the Puncher had said to him; he saw the common sense of it, but it was not, he felt, possible for him. He could not get away from his mates.

The Puncher stuck to him. One evening he took Joe back with him to his home.

" I shall never forget that night," says Joe, with profound feeling.

There was no vision, no conversion. I expected to hear that Puncher had got him to pray, and that the vision had come. No. What the poor hunted, harried, and desperate criminal will never forget is the brightness and happiness of the Puncher's home.

"And he took *me* there!" says Joe, opening his eyes; "me, fresh from prison, and bad if ever a man was bad. I shall never forget that evening."

But before the Puncher could proceed with his humanizing, Joe was back in prison.

This time he prayed to God nearly every night of his sentence, and this time it was not for death.

A new idea had come to the criminal. He was persuaded that if he could get a good woman to marry him he would be able to live a straight life. With this fixed idea in his head, this desperate terror of the police knelt down in his prison cell night after night, and prayed that God would give him a wife. Among all the strange behests that go into the infinite from the souls of kneeling mortals, this human cry of the burglar in prison must seem to some the very strangest—for he was praying for his idea of a Saviour, the only Saviour who could help him, a good woman—" that not impossible She."

When he came from his praying and his prison labour, he found the faithful Puncher wating for him. This time the Puncher begged him to come straight to the Salvation Army hall, but the Criminal said no to that, and went on his way. If there was a God, He would answer that prayer of the prison cell, and send a woman to save him.

A night or two after there was a dispute in a public-house. The two disputants adjourned to fight it out. One of them was Joe. He nearly killed his man, but he himself suffered frightfully —his head was half split, his cheeks were cut, and his face was so smashed about that he was scarcely recognizable. He went from the fight to a chemist's shop and had his head bandaged, his wounds dressed. While this was being done, he felt the hopelessness of his case—his own utter hopelessness, and the strength of the net of crime which held him like a bird. He went straight from the bandaging to the hall of the Salvation Army.

At first no one recognized him. He sat there, with his bruised and blackened eyes, his swollen lips, and his bandaged head, listening to what they had to say. Then one of the Salvationists came to him, recognized him, and said:

" Aren't you tired of your life? "

" I am."

" Wouldn't you like to begin again? "

" I would."

Then followed the usual invitation, and Joe got up and marched to the penitent form. He knelt down, and some of them knelt beside him. They counselled him. They prayed for his soul. He got up saying that he was saved.

What happened nobody knows. Joe himself is unable to explain. He knelt there and prayed; he rose feeling that he had sufficient strength to make a fight for a clean life. He says he felt himself quite free of the net of crime.

Subconscious mentation? The working of the mind, fed by a suggestion from the Puncher? Yes, this is quite a likely theory; but why the man should go to his prayers straight from a fight, why his head singing with blows should hold the idea of prayer, and should be capable of receiving peace—this is difficult to explain. More difficult, too, the explanation of his complete conversion, the instant and complete conversion of a criminal called habitual—so that he rose up with no desire to steal, and, as the sequel has proved, with strength to withstand the temptation of his former associates, with courage to march in the very streets frequented by those men under the banner of a ridiculed salvation.

Even the Puncher could not believe that the Criminal was completely saved. He said to the adjutant, with anxiety, " I'm not happy about Joe; I can't help thinking he ought to have another dip." To begin with, Joe had never done a day's work in his life. It was difficult to see how he would accustom himself to daily toil for a small wage; and he showed no particular enthusiasm in his conversion.

But Joe was waiting for his prayer to be answered.

They got him employment in a laundry. He received no wages at first, only his food, but he worked well and never once gave occasion for anxiety. The whole neighbourhood marvelled to see this cracksman, this friend of Milsom and Fowler, at humble work.

One day he was painting a cart, and looking up from his job saw a girl looking at him. He felt that his prayer was answered. He felt convinced that this was the wife for whom he had prayed.

He managed to strike up an acquaintance, albeit diffident of himself and terribly conscious of his bad record.

One day, when they were friends, and had discussed many things, including their ideas of a happy home, Joe said to her, " Do you think you could marry a man like me? "

" I don't know," she answered.   " Why? "

" Because when I was in prison," he said, " I asked God to give me a wife, and I can't help thinking you are the one."

But before she could reply, all that he had been crowded on his mind, and he compared himself with this good, pure, sensible girl, and felt unworthy.   He told her all this, and said that while he could not help asking her to be his wife, he did not expect that she would marry him.   He frankly and finely said that he might drift back and be what he was.

The girl said, " I know the risk.   But I tell you what.   I'll marry you, providing you join the Army and become a regular soldier."

Was that the moment of Joe's conversion?

It was at that moment he felt suddenly and supremely exalted; his poor troubled soul was flooded with light, like an answer to prayer, and he felt assured that he was under the mercy and protection of a God Who cared.   " How happy I was!—and how happy I am! " he exclaimed.

It is interesting or surprising, as you like it, to see the part played by the Salvation Army in this man's love story.   The girl wanted a security. In all London she knew no other than the Salvation Army. If he became a soldier, she would become his wife. The very poor, swept by an ocean of irresistible oppugnance, have a refuge. It is the Salvation Army.

This man—one of our habitual criminals—is now as much respected in the neighbourhood where he was once the chief terror, as any man living a good, honest, and unselfish life. His devotion to his wife is an adoration. And people laugh when they tell you about Joe's tenderness to children, and how he loves to nurse a baby.

It seems to me that at the back of this conversion is the force we call, rather slightingly, respectability. The man wanted to be respectable, wanted a home, wanted to be free of prisons and police, wanted to have a Sunday dinner and a clean conscience. Well, but what is all this except a desire to be better than he was, to be consciously right, superior, and happy, to reach the height of his character?

After all, respectability is only another name for desire for betterment. And it must be seen that his conversion did not stop at respectability. He is supremely happy after three years of married life; he works for his living; it is a job to make both ends meet; there is sometimes an anxiety about the future; but in the midst of this happiness, respectability, and harassing anxiety, the soul of the Criminal is directed, like that of the Puncher, to saving other souls. He is one of the Salvationists in that bad neighbourhood who works with all his main to convert the wicked, the evil, and the profitless, and quite simply, quite genuinely, without fee or reward, and with a fine manful earnestness he talks bravely to the worst of his former companions about the love of God.

If respectability is the cause, the fruits of respectability in the character of this criminal are the fruits of religion.

# VI

## A COPPER BASHER

WHEN he was fourteen years of age he deliberately left a comfortable home and gave himself to the London streets. From earliest childhood he had manifested what is said to be the unmistakable trait of a criminal —resistance to educative influence. Now, in the full lustihood of boyhood, he went to the streets. He went deliberately. He liked them. He wanted them. There appeared to be no power which could train him for social life.

It is interesting that this thoroughly bad and criminal man has never been the slave of sensual appetites. He has never smoked, he never had the smallest desire for tobacco, has never even been anxious enough to make experiment of this habit. Again, he has never been a drinker. Public-houses have been useful to him in the way of business; he has made them *rendezvous* for the concocting of crimes; but he has never had the least craving for alcohol. As regards other sensual temptations, he appears always to have been equally immune.

One powerful passion possessed his being from childhood, and left no room for anything else;

this was the passion for crime. And, not crime on the grand scale, not valorous burglary nor carefully projected forgery or murder, but mean, savage, beastly, cowardly, and odious crime. The reader is now making the acquaintance of a human monster who occupied a middle place between the felon and the hooligan; a man despised by the great criminal and feared by the rough—a ruffian and a cur.

He sits before me, talking of his past crimes in a way that makes me shudder. I do not know any man who has at times so filled me with loathing and aversion. He is short of stature, with great breadth of high shoulders, the brief neck fat and spongy. His hair is black and grows in a silly fringe over his forehead; his heavy face is the colour of dough; there is deadness to human feeling in the blue eyes; the cruel mouth, which is never closed, shows teeth which never meet, and has a tired expression, a little contemptuous and indifferent. He speaks in the manner of one whose tongue is too big for the mouth, thickly, slowly, drawlingly. Sometimes he laughs, and the sound is thin, heartless, metallic. The impression he makes upon me is one of horror.

And yet the mind of the man compels interest. One feels that here is an aspect of the human soul full of extraordinary suggestion. He gives one fresh ideas concerning evil. He makes iniquity take new shapes before the mind. One contemplates him with curiosity and baffled wonderment.

His family is of Irish origin. The father and mother were respectable people occupying a more or less decent house, and following as well as they could the religion of their forefathers, a Roman Catholic priest occasionally visiting them in their home and encouraging them in ordinary respectability. The brothers and sisters responded to this training. They went obediently to school, they attended church, they said their prayers, they grew up with the idea of getting the best employment they could, and submitted, without question, to the routine of civilization, and the necessities of their situation in the social world.

Danny was the black sheep of this humble family. He was like a stone to his schoolmasters, imbibing nothing, and indifferent to chastisement. He played truant from church. He refused to say his prayers. He regarded the whole life of the home with contemptuous disfavour. Never once, he says, was he conscious of any desire to learn, to be good, to work and get on in the world. Always, from his earliest remembrance, he resented discipline and loathed effort. He regarded both with impatient contempt. Why should one be careful of behaviour? Why should one try to get on? The whole of his being supplied no answer to these questions.

At the age of fourteen the home-life became insufferable. Its monotony irked him. He hated it and despised it. Although in that home he was assured of a comfortable bed and a sufficiency of food, he preferred the hazard of the streets. He went out one day with his hands in his empty pockets, and he never returned.

He became a slinking animal of prey, a human stoat, with the streets of London for his hunting-ground. His great physical strength made him welcome to a gang of youths who had taken to the streets, most of them at any rate, on account of brutality and starvation at home. This gang lived by crime, and were seldom so hard put to it as to sleep in the open. Their headquarters was a common lodging-house. Danny, who knew them all, and had often joined them in their deviltries, announced to them his intention of living free. They welcomed him gladly. He became their leader.

When this gang had made enough money by crime for food and lodging, they would turn, for diversion, to the local hooligans, and use them brutally. The Londoner who wanders into the poor quarters may often have noticed a gang of vagabond young men hurrying through the streets as though with some definite and pressing purpose in view. He may, perhaps, have thought them to be hooligans. In reality they were probably the dreaded enemies of hooligans, young criminals whose passion for savagery drives them every now and then to fight those for whom the police do not trouble to interfere. Apparently, a young criminal is often visited with this overmastering impulse to fight, and as soon as he has earned enough money for his needs and has eaten his fill, an hour's idleness at a street corner will end in one of these sudden sallyings out to fight the roughs.

Danny took part in endless battles of this kind, many and many a time half murdering his enemies. It was his sport—his cricket and football and physical culture. The gang to which he belonged was powerful, savage, and desperate. Nobody dared to interfere with it. Let Danny and his mates swing suddenly round a street corner, and women drew back from the gate to the doorsteps, children were called from the gutters, and the hooligans ran for their lives. During the fight, men looked on from the doors and windows of the houses, never daring to interfere, even if their own sons were among the hooligans. And this was merely the recreation of Danny and his gang of thieves.

This savagery took another form when Danny advanced in strength and brutality. It was a favourite occupation of theirs to waylay a policeman at night, to club him from behind with a piece of iron, and while he lay unconscious and silent on the ground to kick him from head to heel.

Danny became what is called a " Copper Basher."

Perhaps this cowardly scoundrelism was inspired by hatred of prison. Very soon after Danny had taken to the streets he was arrested for felony, and disappeared from society for three months. His crime, of which he will not speak, and which he proudly insists was a " felony," may possibly have been the theft of twopence or threepence from a child sent to fetch a loaf of bread from the baker's. Whatever it was, Danny went to prison for three months, and those three months made him infinitely more cruel, infinitely more savage, infinitely more dangerous than ever he had been before. Three years might have broken his heart, three months hardened it.

A few instances of the way in which he earned his living will suffice to give the reader an idea of his mind. As a boy he learned to let a mate snatch his cap from his head and fling it among the boxes displayed outside a grocer's or a fruiterer's shop; while the mate ran away in pretended fear of Danny, Danny, apologizing to the shopman, would recover his cap with an egg or an apple, or a pound of sausages inside it, and rush off to punish his accomplice. Later on he became an expert shop-lifter. For months, even for years, one may say that this man lived by stealing from shops. He was not content with snatching goods, but coveted the money in the till. This

was one of his favourite dodges: He and a mate,
having chosen their shop, and seen that it was
empty, would enter swiftly from the street; while
Danny vaulted the counter and filled his pockets
from the till, the other lay full length in front
of the door leading to the parlour; if by chance
Danny was so long at the till as to give the
shopman time to rise from his chair, on opening
the door and rushing out upon the thief, the unfortunate tradesman would trip over the accomplice's body, and come a cropper.

It can be imagined that blackguards of this type
would soon discover the shops kept by poor old
women with no man to protect them.

Another very profitable " lay " was that of
stealing from drunken men. It did not matter
whether the drunkard was a poor man or a rich
man, whether he was discovered by day or by
night; Danny always went for him and left him
bare. One story, illustrating the coldbloodedness
of these young criminals, will show the reader
how calmly robberies of this order can be exe-
cuted in the streets.

One night, ranging the better quarters of London in search of prey, Danny and a mate noticed
a well-dressed man sitting on the doorstep of a
house in one of the best London squares. They
immediately made for him, and found him sound
asleep. There were people in the neighbourhood,
but not near them. They took the man's money,

his pocketbook, his watch and chain, his studs and links, and handkerchief. During these operations he roused, and they mothered him with great tenderness, professing their willingness to see him safely home. Then, when the robbery was complete, they looked about them. No one was to be seen. The man was quiescent, dozing back into huddled sleep. Will it be believed that these two savages turned round, set about the man they had robbed, and half murdered him with their fists and boots—out of sheer deviltry? The man was an Irishman, and a wild one; he made an attempt to fight; and even when smashed and kicked and broken he collapsed on the ground, he still kept up a gurgling shout for help. The two blackguards walked quietly away, their hands in their pockets. At the corner of the square they encountered a policeman. "Gov'nor," said Danny, with a cheerful smile, "there's a wild Irishman down there, mad drunk; it'll take two of you to hold him."

Another story illustrates the depravity of this type of mind in another aspect. From all I can gather the popular notion is not altogether true that there is honour among thieves. Thieves prey upon each other, give each other up to the police, rob and steal from each other. Certainly the type of thief represented by Danny never experiences a single scruple. That is what makes this man's story so interesting. He was of brutes

the most brutal, of savages the most savage, of
liars and traitors the most lying and the most
treacherous; and throughout it all he never once
felt that he was doing anything base or mean—
the more mean, indeed, the more it tickled his
fancy. He did the most scurvy things imaginable
without a moment's twinge of conscience, and
laughed over them afterwards.

What does the reader think of minds capable
of such a scheme as this? The story got about
that a bad woman had " pinched " a purse and
was treating two of her friends in a public-house.
Two thieves immediately set out to get the stolen
purse. When they reached the public-house, one
of them boldly asked for a share of the plunder.
It was refused. He then told the other two
women by signs that it meant five shillings each
if they cleared out. They emptied their tumblers,
and departed—with loving farewells to the be-
mused friend who had " treated " them. When
they were outside, the thief filled himself a glass
of water, grabbed the purse, passed it to his mate,
and at the same time flung the water full in the
face of the woman as she rose to pursue. The
water struck her in the mouth, and she stumbled
back choking; the thief filled another tumbler and
shot the water, with tremendous force, between
her gasping lips, sending her down. While she
lay on the floor, he poured more water down her
mouth and over her face. Then he calmly called

the landlord. "Here's a woman in a fit," he
said; "give us some more water." The landlord
hastily passed a heavy carafe, and the thief poured
it over the woman till she was nearly suffocated.
"She'll be all right in a minute or two," said
the thief, and got up. The woman staggered to
her feet, choking and purple, and made her
way out of the house in a vain quest of the
thief.

Danny laughs over that story to this day, and I
do not think that even now, while he hates the
act and could not do it again, he realizes the full
measure of its cruelty and abomination.

But while he was following a life of crime, living with criminals in common lodging-houses, and
never doing an hour's honest work, there came
constant and increasingly long interruptions from
the police. Again and again Danny was arrested, again and again the police got even with
him in the cell at the station, and again and again
he "went up the street." If he laughs at the
memory of his crimes, he laughs good-naturedly
at the punchings and kickings which the police
gave him in the cell. He says he never got so
knocked about in his life. "They'd punch me
in the nose," he says, smiling; "and when I
went down wallop, one of them would hold me
up for his pal to have a smack at my mouth.
And then they'd all set about me with their boots.
Cruel!" he says, tossing his head and laughing

good-temperedly.    He calls these private punishments of the police " having it done upon me."

Of course, Danny was well known as a cowardly assaulter of police.    One understands that
retribution in the cell of the station.    But it was
not the way to make this savage enemy of
society a useful and a virtuous citizen.    Every
time Danny " came down the street " he was
worse.

" I'll tell you what prison does for a man."
Danny leans forward, rests both forearms on the
table, and regards me fixedly, with bitterness evident in his loose mouth.    " It hardens him.    Ask
any man who has done time.    I don't care who it
is, nor what his offence was, nor whether he was
hard or green when he went in.    It's bound to.
It can't do no otherwise.    It hardens a man."
He sits back, and continues in his drawling voice.
" Another thing it does is to learn a man more
tricks than what he knew before he went in.
Prisons see more thieving in one day than the
rest of the world sees in a fortni't.    It stands to
reason.    Lock up a lot of men, treat them like
animals, half starve them, and never make any
attempt to teach them, and what's the result?
They do you all round.    You'd never believe how
much plug tobacco gets into prison.    There's
precious few warders who don't do a bit of private
trading on their own account.    And the cook-
shop tempts starving men, and sharpens their

wits. Well, I learnt more clever dodges in prison than ever I learned outside, I know that."

Certainly the moral instructions had no effect upon his conscience. Like others I have questioned, this man tells me that never once in all the long record of his prison experience did a chaplain enter his cell or speak to him in private. Never once did a single person, governor or chaplain, make any effort to awaken and stimulate the sleeping conscience of this criminal. As a representative of society the governor received him, and locked him up; as a representative of religion the chaplain read prayers and preached a sermon to him on Sunday. The taxpayer in his home, confidently hoping that the poor wretches in prison are being reformed and regenerated, likes to think that posterity will escape the heavy charge of punishing the lawbreakers. And in his cell Danny plots more villainies and rehearses new crimes against the hour when he will go " down the street."

Once only did Danny ever have private words with a prison chaplain. After serving a term he went before the chaplain, who had expressed no wish to see him, and asked for the suit of clothes provided by the Prisoners' Aid Society. The chaplain looked at him, shook his head, and replied, " Not for you. You'll be back again in a week or two." Like the Criminal whose story we have told, Danny's blood fired up. But he checked. "That's giving a bloke a good heart to go down the road with!" he exclaimed, and laughed. If the representative of religion could have realized it, that laugh was his indictment.

Consider, in passing, how the story of this chaplain illustrates the truth of Professor James's remarks about second-hand religion. Directly you put a man within a gaol, as the official representative of religion, as the official deputy obeying the divine injunction to visit those in prison, be sure that Christianity becomes there as much a matter of routine as the rest of the penal discipline. One has sympathy with the chaplain; to visit hardened, ignorant, and perhaps abusive criminals all the day long is a dreary work; but one has no sympathy with those of them at any rate who, being paid to do this saving work, stay at home saying that it is useless. I do not think that any reasonable man believes an official representative of religion capable of accomplishing the regeneration of criminals; while a great number will perhaps hold the view that missions to prisoners, conducted by missionaries who have themselves suffered and repented, might make religion even in a prison the true and vital thing which saves the soul.

Danny, as I have said, represents the lowest type of criminal. When one reflects upon the utter baseness of his mind it seems impossible that he should ever have turned from his wickedness and lived.  Before telling how that happened, I must narrate an incident of his prison career which will show how very base and vile was his character.

Have you ever thought that a prison warder may suffer from nerves?  I remember some years ago going over the prison at Wormwood Scrubbs and seeing a single warder, unarmed, in charge of a number of men in the carpenter's shop all handling more or less formidable tools; it struck me, then, that a good story might be written of a convict whose eyes succeeded in breaking down a warder's nerves, so that he dared not to be alone.  Danny told me of an incident that shows my imagination had reason.

" There was a warder," he said, " who got the jumps and tried to cure them by being extra strict.  He was particularly funky of one man.  Somehow or other, I was always a favourite with the warders, got soft jobs, and was treated lenient.  Well, this bloke came to me one day and said, ' Look here, if you'll say that so-and-so,' naming the man he was afraid of, ' set about me, it'll be worth something good to you.'  I said I wouldn't say nothing of the kind; but sure enough the prisoner was put away.  When I was taken before the governor, and he said that I had behaved well in rescuing the warder from the prisoner, that the poor man might probably have been murdered but for me, and that in consideration of this

act he would see that my sentence was shortened,
I was so taken aback that I couldn't speak."

One feels that Danny might have spoken if he
had chosen; one does not believe that he ever lost
power of speech or was ever astonished by anything.   No; he was the type of man who would
" give anyone away."   But Danny is ashamed of
certain things in his past; the farther he gets
away from that past and the more settled he becomes in happiness and peace of soul, the more is
he inclined to blurr the blackest things in his
memory.   He tells you his first crime was a
" felony "; he prefers that you should form the
impression of a terrible burglary, not pence-
snatching from a poor child.   He says he was
taken aback so that he could not speak; he does
not want you to think that he gave a man away.
If he lies in this way, one can forgive him.

I am convinced, from what I have heard, that
this man had in his soul all that is most dastardly,
base, scurvy, and vile; I do not think there was
any imaginable mean thing that he would not
have done.   And the more one realizes this utter
and horrible baseness, the more wonderful appears the revolution of his character.

It came about that Danny was arrested and
sentenced to a long term of imprisonment soon
after the conversion of the Puncher.   Of course,
he had heard of that miraculous event, and, of
course, he had laughed over it with some of the

Puncher's old mates in the lodging-houses. But in prison, realizing the weary time of monotonous suffering ahead of him, the conversion of the Puncher stuck in his mind and haunted his thoughts. He knew that the Puncher was better off as a saved man than as a drunkard. He imagined the Puncher's home, his fare, his good meals, nice clothes, his liberty unshadowed by fear of police. Then he considered within himself how bad and low the Puncher had been, a " hopeless " drunkard. It seemed to him a wonderful thing that a man so abandoned to drink, and such a man, should all of a sudden give it up. He was quite dazed and staggered by the thought. What a drunkard, what a frightful drunkard, the Puncher had been; and now he was clean and respectable!

For days the prisoner fed his mind upon this thought in the solitude of his cell. Alone in that little cramped space of stone, locked in, and without sight of tree, sky, or moving creature, the hardened criminal reflected upon the " fair marvel " of Puncher's conversion.

And one day revelation came to this base and savage mind. It came suddenly, without miracle, and it did not in the least stagger him. He started up with the thought in his mind, " If God can save Puncher, He can save me! "

The revelation was too clear and staring to stagger him. This thing which had never before occurred to him, was obvious, plain as a pike-staff. And yet it was wonderful. " If God can save Puncher, that awful and degraded sinner, He can save me—I who love myself and know, therefore, that I am not so bad as other people." Why on earth had he not thought of this before?

In Victor Hugo's *Quatre-Vingt-Treize* there is this question and answer: Boisberthelot said to La Vieuville, " Do you believe in God, chevalier? " La Vieuville replied, " Yes. No. Sometimes."

Sometimes all men believe. Danny's " sometimes " had now arrived. Hitherto God had never occupied his mind. He had thought nothing about religion, one way or the other. " God " was a term convenient to round off an oath with. " Hell " meant something bad. As for " heaven," it was too soft even for an oath; he had never been interested in that place; it seemed to him something unmanly and young-ladylike; he certainly had no objection to going there after death, if hell was the only alternative; but he reckoned it as bad as a Sunday-school.

All these years Danny had lived in modern London, which spends millions of pounds a year on religion and morality, and his ideas of God were what we have said. Surrounded on all sides by churches, charitable agencies, rescue societies, and educational machinery; brought by prison discipline to a willy-nilly consideration of formal

religion on many a crawling sabbath day, this
man had yet never formulated to himself any
ideas of God, existence, immortality.    His phrase
concerning religion has a penetrating significance:
" I never gave it a thought."    He had thoughts,
plenty of them, for crime, scoundrelism, and lowest rascality; but not one, not one, for life, its
meaning, its responsibility, its great issue.

And now the first idea of God which occurred
to his mind was that of a Rescuer, some indefinable Power capable of turning his unhappiness
into happiness.    Without any question as to the
ability of this Something to help and save, Danny
surrendered himself.    But in a manner characteristic of the man.    If the phrase may pass, this
wretched prisoner put God on His mettle.    And
there was an element of self-righteousness in his
idea.    " If God can save Puncher, He can save
me."

To reach God, he understood, prayer was necessary.    So he got upon his knees in the prison cell,
and offered his first prayer.    He was a young
man, and twelve whole years out of his short life
had been passed in gaols; he had never had an
opportunity of understanding religion; he had
never given the idea of God a moment's thought.
But he knew just enough of the matter to kneel.
In what spirit he knelt one cannot exactly say;
the important fact is that this depraved brute
did kneel, and did pray.

He says that he prayed throughout his long sentence, and *hoped* that when he left prison fortune would smile upon him, that it would be " all right."

He came out and was met by the Puncher. An answer to prayer.

The Puncher talked to him in his quiet, sensible fashion. What a rotten life he was living! Life passing, middle age approaching, and twelve years of prison! Was the game worth the candle? Was he happy?

Now this reasoning is powerful enough, because so obvious and sensible, in the case of a drunkard; but Danny was a man without carnal appetites; he was a brain concentrated on crime. Could it *convert* the *thought* of this man, could it change the grey matter of his brain, habituated from infancy to cunning and rascality? Its one effect was to draw from Danny the admission that certainly he did not want to be " copped " again.

Then the Puncher moved from morality to religion. He spoke of spiritual peace, the pleasant feeling of a life lived rightly, the power of God to wipe away sins and give a soul a new birth. He told Danny that there was no other way.

Danny was impressed. He said he wanted to be saved. He said he wouldn't mind giving religion a chance. But, what about work? He

would have to work; that wasn't nice to begin
with; and, where was he to find it?

Puncher said, " Leave that to God."

The answer was a fine one; it manifested a profundity of spiritual experience.   For the Puncher
knew that while in his present state Danny was
incapable of prolonged and monotonous work, and
was inclined to give himself to religion only to
escape prison and get a " soft job "; nevertheless,
let him be converted and his whole attitude to
work and to religion would suffer a revolutionary
change.   Let him be converted, and he would welcome any work, the most arduous and dreary, so
long as it was honest; let him be converted, and
he would rather starve than live by the religion
which had given him such pure joy.

Such was the Puncher's faith in conversion; such to him was the reality of the new
birth.

And this is really what happened to Danny.

Danny came to the Salvation Army meeting;
he felt a light of illumination break through his
soul at the adjutant's assurance of God's *love* for
the worst of men; he realized all of a sudden the
need for love in his own barren heart, and in
that spirit—the spirit of a broken and contrite
heart—he knelt at the penitent form, and for the
first time really reached into the infinite.   He
prayed for mercy; he prayed for strength.

He rose from his knees a changed man.

This change was absolute and entire. From being cruel, he became as tender as a woman. From being a cunning thief, he became scrupulously honest. From being a loafer and unemployable, who had never done a single day's work in his civil life, he became an industrious workman. From being basely selfish, he became considerate for others, giving both himself and presently his money to the service of religion. " The greatest change in Danny," said a friend who knows him well, " is his gentleness. He couldn't hurt a fly now, and any tale of cruelty or suffering, especially where children are concerned, fairly breaks him down." What a revolution in personality! What a new birth!

Danny has risen to be foreman in his employment, trusted and respected by his masters, and obeyed by those under him with the scrupulousness which inferior natures observe in their relations with a powerful will. He has married a religious woman, who would only accept his proposal on condition of his remaining always a soldier in the Salvation Army, and they both work for the Army, heart and soul, in their spare time. The home is one of the happiest in the district; Danny's bargaining in the matter of old furniture astonishing the whole neighbourhood. Such muslin curtains in the windows, such flower-boxes on the sills, such carpets, pictures, easy chairs, and mantelpiece ornaments, are not to be matched for miles around.  " Oh, yes," said one of his friends; " he's a daddy for home."

In spite of his appearance, which repels me, in spite of his manner, which repulses me, this once low brute has reached from vileness to goodness, and is a force on the side of religion.  He loves his children very tenderly, he would no more whine or cadge than maltreat a drunken man, and he is never too tired to do a service, never unwilling to help in any good and noble work. Conversion has not altered his appearance or his manner; but it has given him a new soul.

Let this incident show to what point in spirituality such a base nature may be brought by religion.  Not long ago one of his sisters, a flaming Roman Catholic, who seems to loathe her brother more now for his Salvationism than ever she did for his crimes, came to the open-air Sunday meeting of this corps, openly reviled and mocked her brother before the whole street, and finally struck him a stinging blow across the mouth.

All that Danny did was to cross to the other side of the ring.  His look was very ugly; he was as white as a sheet, his eyes hardened and expressed that which almost frightened some people; but he restrained himself, held his peace, and kept his hands off the virago.

When you think what this man had been, you realize the merit of his conduct, and the miracle of his new character.

# VII

## LOWEST OF THE LOW

**M**RS. BURRUP, from the earliest days of her marriage, was fond of a glass. But when her husband died, leaving her with a baby, this fondness changed to a deep and abiding affection. She could earn sufficient money by charing and laundry work to drown her bereavement in drink, and she proceeded to drown it in the company of other lonely women who preferred the spacious atmosphere of a public-house to the pathos of the vacant chair.

On these visits to the tavern she took her baby in her arms, and there the little boy was encouraged to be good and quiet and grateful by having his lips occasionally stroked by a finger dipped in gin. He was still little more than an infant when Mrs. Burrup temporarily divided her fondness for a glass with a second husband, a man who had at least one taste in common with the widow—devotion to a glass. The happy couple drank together, and the child, changed from lap to lap in the public-house, became dimly aware of some alteration in the physical universe —tasting now the finger of his mother, and now the finger of his stepfather.

When he was old enough to understand things, he perceived that the prevailing character of human life was trouble. The relations between his mother and stepfather were strained. From morning to night the voices of these two grown-ups were in a loud key. Occasionally their arms whirled and one of them would fall to the floor, rising with a reddened eye to shout fierce-sounding words after the departing figure of the other. The child had some knowledge of what whirling arms signified. Occasionally he came in for a cuff, a shaking, or a peremptory smacking. Later, the boy discovered that he was generally hungry. This discovery swallowed up interest in all other phenomena. He was quite young when he learned to look after the cravings of his own stomach. He did not steal, as so many boys in poor London do steal, merely for the sake of adventure and the love of danger, but rather in the rude, barbaric, and honest fashion of our ancestors, to satisfy the demands of his body. He stole persistently. This poor little ragged child, slinking through the crowded streets of the metropolis, was like a famished animal hunting for prey. He hunted for his food. The well-fed members of a Hunt can have no idea, following hounds, of the real excitement of a chase. The little boy, creeping up to shop doors, or diving in and out of costermongers' barrows, with a sharp eye for policemen, and a gnawing wolf in his stomach, could have told them what hunting actually is. He was fox and hound; he experienced the dangers, delights, and difficulties of running with the hare and hunting with the hounds. He hunted food and was hunted by society. It is not to be expected that a little ignorant, hungry boy could prey upon respectable and law-abiding tradesmen with impunity, could outwit the watchfulness and sagacity of that immense force which society has raised for its protection against thieves, villains, pariahs, and outcasts. Again and again the poor little creature was laid by the heels—that is to say, had the lobe of an ear caught between the thumb and index of a policeman, and found himself marched thus ignominiously home to the buckle-end of his stepfather's strap. If he managed to elude the police, seldom a day went by when some watchful young tradesman at his shop door did not " fetch him a crack on the head," just as a warning not to steal from that particular shop.

The boy's life consisted of more kicks than halfpence. He was one of those shivering, dirty, and neglected little creatures who creep about the streets on naked feet, with the rain wetting their mat of hair, and the wind driving at their ragged jackets—forlorn, famished, and wretched. This little pale, blue-lipped, shivering child was more like a homeless dog than a mother's son. If someone had caught him early in those cruel days, had taken him from that wicked environment, taught him habits of cleanliness and self-respect, given him some idea of good and honour, placed him in a position where he could see life as a pleasant thing, and reasonably understand the metaphor which calls Providence a Father, he might have grown into a manhood worthy of civilization and religion; he might have been saved from infamy.   But no one, except the police, took notice of this little child.   None of the numerous charitable agencies to which humanity subscribes what it can afford out of its plenty, discovered this waif, rescued this stray, saved this outcast.   Beaten by a drunken stepfather, neglected by a drunken mother, kicked and cuffed by tradesmen, hunted and arrested by the police— always dirty, always hungry, always afraid, this mite in the midst of vast London was utterly without friend or helper, utterly alone with the wolf gnawing at his vitals.   Is it not terrible to think that we can devise nothing to save such suffering as this?

He was caught at a bad piece of stealing when he was just beginning his teens, and was taken to the police-station like a criminal, locked up in a cell, and tried on the following morning by a magistrate in the police-court.   His sentence was six months in a reformatory school.

Either the methods of that school were not good, or the boy's bad habits had struck too deep a root in his character. He did not at any rate encounter such affection or deep interest in his career as to turn his heart. He left the school better fed and better clothed than when he entered it, and he certainly returned home with some faint notion of discipline and order. But his heart was not touched.

Miserable in his home, sick of himself and his own freedom, he left his parents at the age of sixteen, and after wandering about the world till he was dead hungry, dead tired, and dead wretched, enlisted as a soldier. He welcomed the army as a sure and fairly decent " doss." He had clothes, a bed, almost enough food for his needs, and sufficient at the end of a week to buy a drink. He put up with the drills and discipline for these advantages. As for fighting patriotism, honour of the regiment, and martial glory of a soldier's career, he thought no more about those things than any anarchist in Soho.

But as the monotony of a soldier's life more and more soured on his stomach, he took more and more to his mother's comfort in widowhood, and became a hard drinker. The little boy who had hunted for food in the London streets was now a tall and bony man, six feet in height, small of head, with a fierce and quarrelsome face always aflame with alcohol. Continually he found himself in trouble over drunkenness, but he bore his punishment without shame or regret, not having the smallest ambition to rise in the service. However, as drink laid an ever stronger hold upon him, he more and more relaxed his hold upon himself, he more and more resented discipline, correction, and punishment. He became choleric, mutinous, and fierce. His temper was every day more out of control. When he was not in trouble with his officers he was in trouble with his messmates. He had the world against him, knew it, and opposed the world to the extent of his poor disdain and the fierceness of his anger.

At the end of five years' troubled soldiering he had a dispute with a corporal. Voices rose, words became violent. In the heat of this argument the corporal fell back upon authority. He gave his antagonist an order. The soldier refused to obey it; he was drunk, and the command of a smaller man goaded his rage to madness. The corporal threatened. At last the drunken soldier seized up his rifle, and swearing that he would murder the other, made so good an attempt that he was arrested, tried, and sentenced to six months hard labour, and given " his ticket "— that is to say, discharged with ignominy.

When he came out of prison and found himself at large in the civilian world, he was wise enough to look about for employment before making a return to settled drinking. He got a decent job in some waterworks, with fair wages, but took to drinking immediately he felt himself certain of wages at the end of the week.   He hated his work.   He appears to have been constitutionally incapable of finding pleasure or interest in any employment.   He honestly disliked all physical exertion.   It irked him, irritated him, bored him. But nothing really pleased him, except drink. Life did not interest him in the least.   He drank, as his mother before him, to drown his sorrow, to forget life.   What a world!—where it is necessary for a man to go to work six days out of seven.

This man was weighed down by an immense ennui.

Drink lost him this good employment, and he went from the waterworks to a distillery—a change for the worse, from water to whisky.   It was not long before drunkenness lost him this second job, and in a tipsy rage at being dismissed he had a row with the police, and was sent to prison for three months.

When he came out from prison he descended to the depths of infamy.

It is impossible, in this book, to tell the story of his life at this point of his career.   It can only be hinted.   Coming out of prison in rebellion against the world, determined that never again would he do a day's work, Burrup went to a public-house, where he fell in with a woman earning her own living by evil ways.   He does not appear to have realized at once, or to have contemplated

for some time, the nature of the proposal made to
him by this woman.  He was attractive, and he
thought she admired him.  He knew that she was
aware of his homeless condition; he thought that
her invitation to lodge with her was just the
woman's kindness, born of admiration.  He accepted it, and for some days lodged in that
fashion.  Then he found himself provided with
money by this woman.  A little later, and he was
called in to assist her in her business.  Of a
sudden he found himself the lowest of men.

Did his conscience ever smite him?  Yes.  To
this extent: when the woman's earnings were not
sufficient for their needs he went out and thieved
for her.  That was all.  Apparently he soon got
over the contempt which even low people in low
neighbourhoods openly show for such men.  He
avoided the half-decent population, and consorted
with men engaged in the same horrible para-
sitism.  All this time he was drinking hard, lying
late in bed, and lounging in public-houses.

Presently he seems to have contracted a spirit
of bravado.  He became definitely and resolutely
a criminal.  He found crime a sport.  He went
out into the streets, not as a hungry boy, but as a
thirsty man, and set himself to make money without work, for very joy of the undertaking.  He
was drinking hard, and his brain seemed to be
on fire with criminal ideas.  He supported his
mistress in this fashion for some time; but was

soon a marked man, and therefore from that moment was in trouble with the police. He was arrested, time and again, and always he made such a fight of these arrests that it took as a rule six constables to strap him down on the ambulance and get him to the station. Once, when they caught him stealing boots, he so " bashed " the police about that the mounted patrol had to be called, and he was tied to the horse and dragged all the way to the station. He was generally half murdered during these arrests, being known as one of the worst " copper bashers " in London. On such a man as he was then only God could have mercy.

Twelve years after his discharge from the army, Burrup looked back on three years of immoral freedom, and nine years of prison. Nine years out of the twelve spent in prison! A bad retrospect. What could the future hold? He began to think. His character and the manner of his life had long been so notorious that everybody in the whole of that neighbourhood knew about him, knew about the woman. Among those who knew, and who thought about him, were the angel-adjutant and the Puncher. They tried to reach his soul, tried to lift him from infamy; but he shook them both off with an angry impatience.

A time came, however, when misery made him willing to hear them. His mistress was in gaol;

he was hungry, thirsty, and ashamed; he was thinking of the nine years out of twelve spent in prison; he was beginning to feel that the future held no hope for him; that his to-morrow meant the prison; that for ever he would be harried and maltreated by the police; he was at last so broken and wretched and defeated as to desire some escape.

He thought about the Puncher. He compared that man's past and present. He saw how marvellous was the change in that life, and brooded upon it. While he was thinking, some force in his brain began quietly urging him to follow the Puncher, to do as he had done, to get religion.

He was aware that no one in the whole of the world could do anything but despise him. He knew that he was vile, degraded, infamous, friendless. He knew that the police were against him, that magistrates were ready to send him to prison with bitter words of contempt, that his physical strength was powerless against the forces of law and order, that his hatred of society was a vain fire in his brain, that he had muddled life and had the whole universe against him. If he told the world that he wanted to live a better life, the world would spurn him. Not a soul would believe him. He had asked his prison visitor, a Roman Catholic priest, during his last term, if someone could not help him to go straight; and he received not only no help, but no

encouragement to desire a better life.   He felt
that there was only one hope for him, the Army
that had made the Puncher a decent good man
with a comfortable home.

That was the illumination of this sunken and
degraded soul.   " I had watched the Puncher's
life, I had seen it running clean and straight; and
I resolved all of a sudden that if God could do
such a miracle as that, I would have a cut at it
too."   The diction is of the smallest moment.
This man's desire to have " a cut at it," trans-
lated into the most wistful phrasing of an ex-
quisite mysticism, would still beggar the words.
The desire was the miracle.   It was a movement
of the soul in the spiritual sphere.   When he felt
a longing to try religion, his soul said, " I will
arise and go to my Father," and he had come to
himself.   His mind, blundering with words and
concerned with material things, must not obscure
for us the hidden movements of his spirit waking
from death, turning to the light and desiring rest.
This man, with all his abomination thick about
him, was subliminally moving towards God.
Whatever the spring of his desire, whatever the
cause of his awakening, he desired to be better;
that is to say, he turned his face to the light.

He went straight to the hall of the Salvation
Army, sat by himself at the back of the room,
listened to the hymns, prayers, and readings,
heard the preaching and the invitation, rose from

his seat, marched to the platform, knelt down at the penitent form, and said in a low voice, " God be merciful to me a sinner! "

The past dropped from him like a ragged garment. He was conscious of a great cleansing. A yearning of his soul carried him far away from the hall, the Salvationists, and the congregation of prayerful people. He was caught up into a glowing region of light and intensest satisfaction. Dumb and breathless, he knelt with his face in his hands, conscious only of the radiance, the peace, and the joy. He did not think " I am forgiven," or " I am saved "; he only knew vividly, and yet in a state of dream, that he was at last perfectly happy.

He came out of this ecstasy to the mothering tenderness of the adjutant and the paternal kindness of the Puncher. For the first time in his whole life he was surrounded and supported by pure affection. If the delirious joy of his ecstasy had passed and faded like a dream, at least he was not left alone; he was with good people, who, knowing his old vileness, showed him love; who, knowing the desperate record of his past, showed him trust.

He felt a strength come to his limbs and a power to his mind. He would be worthy of these friends. He said, " I know what has happened to me." They asked him what? He said, " I have been given a second chance."

In a conversation with the adjutant it was decided that he should marry his mistress when she came out of prison, and make it a part of his life's work to save her soul.   The Salvation Army does not make repentance an easy and a pleasant thing; they certainly do not let a man buy an indulgence for his past.   If man or woman comes for salvation, and being saved, confesses to some undiscovered crime, the Army insists upon confession to the wronged person, and to absolute reparation.   This is not done here and there, occasionally; it is a fixed rule; obligatory upon all penitents throughout the world.   Many who come to the penitent form go straight to prison to prove repentance real, suffering for felonies undiscovered and now impossible to discover.

Burrup began his new life by hawking flowers. He got sufficient money to buy two pots of flowers, and walked about the streets till he had sold them.   The purchaser of the last pot, taking compassion on the man, talked to him, and gave him temporary employment.   A lady of title interested in the Army gave him an engagement for six weeks.   In both cases he received the very highest reference for honesty, sobriety, and painstaking industry.

But before his second employment came, he had had his last meeting with the woman.   He and the adjutant went to the prison to receive this poor creature on the threshold of her freedom.

She started at the sight of the Salvationist, and stared first at the adjutant and then at Burrup, silent and perplexed.  The adjutant told her that Burrup had determined to live a clean and respectable life, that he wished to begin that new life by an act of duty, by marrying the woman who had been his mistress, and that before they could become man and wife, it would be well if she would place herself in one of the Salvation Army's homes.

The woman fired up at this suggestion.  She not only resented the idea of entering a home, but mocked Burrup for wishing to marry her. The adjutant pleaded, the woman grew more violent and contemptuous.  It was not until she saw how hopeless was her mission that the adjutant gently reproached the woman for her evil.  At this, curses and blasphemies took the place of contempt.  The adjutant and her convert moved away.  The woman followed them.  Through the crowded streets the convert had to march at the Salvationist's side with this virago following at his heels, shouting out to all the world what he had been, cursing him, spitting on him.  The man endured it, very white of face and grim, without a word.  It would have been easier for some people, perhaps, to face a den of lions.

" I hailed a bus," the adjutant tells me, " compelling her to stay behind, and we left her, feeling that we could not do anything with her, as she was not willing to leave her life of sin." That is the test without which help is of no avail. Until a soul hates evil, little can be done; until it desires good, nothing.

For some little time the woman martyred the poor man struggling to lead a clean and virtuous life. She haunted his lodgings and insulted him in public. She did all she could to drag him down, to break his heart, to drive him mad. But he stuck to his work, suffered her annoyance, and never once looked back.

He set himself another task. This woman refused to let him save her. There was another woman to whom he felt responsible—his mother.

Look quietly and steadily at the effects of conversion, the fruits of repentance, in this man's soul. I think they are worth considering. Remember what he had been, the lowest of the low; consider the privation, destitution, and crime of his earliest childhood; see him as he was all through his life, a thief, pander, bully, and abandoned drunkard; and then mark him after momentary conversion, continuing his hard work, quietly maintaining his honesty and sobriety under the mocking persecution of his former partner in crime, and above all things, setting himself to discover the whereabouts of his mother—that mother to whose neglect he might justly have attributed all the suffering, ignominy, and spiritual ruin of his life—in order that he might save her soul.

The more one thinks about Burrup, the more one apprehends the tremendous power of religion. Conversion did not make him merely a sober and industrious man.   That alone would have been a miracle, for he loved drink as he hated work. But conversion did more for him.   It washed away from his soul at a single stroke all the obstruction of ingrained habits, cleansed him from every impulse of his moral madness, and made him at once tender, loving, considerate, and pure.   He was not content with saving his own soul; conversion would not let him rest in personal security or in flattering self-righteousness; he was driven by the spirit, gladly and rejoicingly, to make others aware of spiritual peace.

And, as we say, he sought out the mother whose neglect in infancy had sown the seeds of all his ruin and disgrace.

He found her in great wretchedness.   The stepfather had abandoned her, and she was exposed to all the privations and cruelties which beset a solitary poor woman at the threshold of old age.   The son told her of his life, told her of his conversion, and asked if she would not come and share his home and his happiness.

This is a new version of the Prodigal Son. Nobler story of its kind, noble in all its simplicity and humility, can hardly be conceived.   This

**prodigal** did not return to the shelter and love of a rich and righteous parent, ready with rewards; but, when he had come to himself, he set out to save that which was lost, set out to offer *his* shelter and *his* love to a bad mother who could only be a load and burden to him; and truly it may be said that when he was a great way off he saw her, and ran and fell upon her neck, and kissed her, so eager and passionate was the desire of his soul to save this woman.

Happiness came to him in the response made by the broken-hearted mother to his offers of affection. She was like one raised from the dead, and clung to her strong son with beseeching and heart-breaking pleadings not to be left again, not to be left in misery and despair. Her cry for forgiveness to him was like a cry to God. The son saved by God, in God's strength saved his mother. In their first embrace, they realized to the full the need for religion, and both experienced at least some of the satisfaction of spiritual peace. Only religion could have saved the son, only religion could have sent the son to save his mother. They had both lived without religion; and they had both suffered. Now, in the awakening of spiritual consciousness, they perceived that only religion made life pure, sweet, and sacred.

She could hardly believe that it was indeed her son who came to lift her up. She could hardly believe that the terrible nightmare of her

dark life had really come to an end.    And she was
like a character in the *Arabian Nights* when he
led her away from her destitution and showed
her the home that his love had prepared for her.
Religion has these earthly enchantments.

Burrup's home is one of the brightest and
happiest in London.    It is full of the decorations
and showiness with which a London workman
loves to manifest both his prosperity and his
domesticity, and all these fine things are kept in
a state of glory by the saved mother, who now
has no thought but of showing her gratitude to
her son with duster and broom, and serving him
all the days of her life.    She is converted to his
religion, and son and mother are as loyally and
devotedly attached to each other as any pair of
human beings in the world.    He loves to put
by his savings to give his mother little treats
and surprises—oh, quite little treats and surprises, for they are poor people; and she on her
part loves to make him some tempting dish for
his supper, and by her labour to keep his linen
and his wardrobe in apple-pie order to show her
gratitude for his love and her own pride in her
son.    They are quite beautiful in their love, and
if Burrup is proud of anything in his life it is
that he can support his mother.

It is long since he was converted, and he has
never married.  Perhaps some memory of the
base past keeps him back, makes him shrink

from offering himself to a good woman.   Or, is it that he really loves his mother more than any-thing in life, and is completely happy in their domestic companionship?

Completely happy?

One thinks that he is not completely happy; that the memory of the past still haunts his peace; and that he will never wholly escape, as he did in the radiance of his conversion, from the black shadow of his dead iniquity.

There are those in the world, to this very day, who like to remind him of what he was.   You have no idea, perhaps, how difficult it is for a man to live out his repentance in poor London.

He said to one of his friends the other day, after talking over the dark days behind him— suddenly drawing himself up to his full height and assuming the look of dignity which becomes his proud, silent, and soldier-like face: " Several would like to see me go back; ah, several!   But there is nothing to go back for.   I know, as God knows, that I am far from perfect.   But—I am better than I used to be."

Do not mistake this clear assertion for self-righteousness.   Burrup said, and says to this day, that his conversion was a second chance.   He does not talk about the love of God.   He thinks that he has yet a long way to go, and he is watch-ing himself.   God has given him a second chance. He stands firm on that conviction, and marks

carefully his conduct under the mercy of this
chance. Quite truthfully and honestly he says,
" I am far from perfect." With a profound gratitude, a London workman's *sursum corda,* he
adds, " I am better than I used to be."

# VIII

## THE PLUMBER

HE made a bad start of life. At the age of six he was running every morning to a public-house for his mother's "livener." To get even with this mother for routing him out of bed before the day was aired, he used to drink some of the beer, occasionally some of the gin. The curiosity of a child's mind may be seen in this, that he arranged these revengeful sips for moments when he would be observed by other children. It was a piece of swagger, as well as the savage action of revenge. Such can be the mind of a child of six.

A recent Act of Parliament has put an end to what was once a common incident of the London streets in early mornings—little half-dressed, bare-legged children creeping along close to the houses with a pot of beer in their hands. Many people have wondered to what ends such children would grow. This is the story of a man who began life in that fashion.

His father was a hard and brutal-minded man, but not a drunkard. His mother, on the other hand, was "addicted to drink." Her addiction began at the moment when she woke from her sleep, it lasted through the day, and was at its fullest power at the hour when publicans close their doors and count their takings. She was one of those women typical of street corners, court entries, and the bench of the public bar. A hat was seldom on her head, her hair hung in a loose knot over her neck, her face—which was fat, pink, soft, and shining—cleaned itself when it felt hot with the dirty end of an apron. She was a big woman, huge-armed, immense in the bosom, broad in the hips, round-shouldered, and firm-necked. There was a sullen savagery in her small eyes, a bitter ferocity in her lips; her voice was harsh, fierce, and vigorous. A typical mother of the London slums thirty years ago, and a type still to be seen among the little white-faced rats and ferrets of the present generation. She did no work. The children were given half-pence to get their meals at barrows, coffee-stalls, and fried-fish shops. This habit of taking one's meals in restaurants has since spread to the fortunate classes, one of many fashions which the upper class has borrowed from the lowest; in the case of this woman the habit grew from a branch of the servant problem, her own constitutional and impatient disgust for domestic work; it is a spirit common in the slums—contempt for work. The father, a navvy, tried to cure his wife of her addiction. He tried with both hands. The impression he made upon her was visible to the naked eye, but the addiction still flourished in the grey matter beyond the reach of fists, hobnails, and straps. Disappointed in the failure of his persuasive powers, and occasionally vexed to find no food in the house, the navvy eased his ruffled feelings by "strapping the kids." He was a man with a troubled brow, a sad eye, and a voice that growled curses on God and human life with a dull monotony. It was not a happy home, and not in the least original. It was one of thousands and thousands of precisely similar homes in London. Cupid, when he descends to the London gutter, appears to delight in the wanton mischief of making these unequal marriages—the sober man yoked to the drunken woman, the drunken man yoked to the sober wife, with always the drunken party in the ascendant. The parents of the man in this story were very like the parents of tens of thousands of children now playing in the streets of London, or carrying their penny for dinner to the gaudy barrow of the Italian vendor of ice-cream.

And I do not think the child was abnormal in the earliness of his cunning. It is common to find quite small infants in shabby districts adept at tricks which in their elders are crimes. This child was naturally quick-witted, intelligent, bright, and humorous. To this day he has the roguish, pleasant face of a comic singer. It struck him as a relief from strappings and other home discomforts to practise sharpness in the world outside. He was one of a great swarm of little hungry, dirty-faced boys wandering through the streets of London looking for what they could pick up. He was a really smart boy when he went out to work, so smart, indeed, as to begin at once making money on his own account. He served a milkman. A very simple facility in sleight-of-hand earned him threepence or fourpence a day. By spilling his dipper as he took the measure from the can, and giving an extra drop afterwards which appeared even more than he spilled, but which was carefully less, he always had milk for sale at the bottom of his can on which his master had no call. In this way he flourished, earned the reputation for being a singularly smart and cheerful boy, and was soon able to get a place in a shop. It was so easy to steal in this place that he was found out. He was sent to prison.

A check of this kind makes some impression on a sensitive boy, however immoral his upbringing. He came out of prison with the idea of never going back there again if he could help it. Reformation having appeared, he was assisted to learn a trade. He was apprenticed to a firm of plumbers and gasfitters.

" Of all the trades in this world," he says, with emphasis, " the plumber's is the *thickest* "; that is to say, the worst from a moral point of view.

" I don't know what it's like now, I hope it's better; if it is, it's a marvel. But my experience is this—there isn't a bigger set of thieves than plumbers. How it comes about, I don't know; carpenters are different, every trade is different, but plumbers seem as if they can't help being what they are, which is hot, and no mistake. I'd as soon have a burglar on my premises any day as a London plumber. That's a strong thing to say, isn't it? That's a rum thing to say of a whole trade? Ah, but it's true."

His first experience of this trade with a bad name was the hardening process. The boy apprentice comes in at once for that brutalizing tyranny which throughout the poorest quarters of London, even among respectable people, seems to regard all politeness, cleanliness, and affection as signs of an evil effeminacy. If you go into any of the London parks, the Regent's, for instance, and stand where poor children are playing in a swarm, you will never hear a sweet or gentle voice. Sisters shout across distance at each other as though they were challenging to a fight: " Come here, can't you? " " Emmy, d'you hear what I say!—come here at once! " " Shut your noise! " " You're a liar! " Cries and calls such as these, and all uttered in voices of ferocity, are the common language of London childhood. And it is only a part of a very wide and potent force in the national character—the hard sternness

which makes the poor endure their miseries in
silence, the unyielding fortitude which supports
them in an abject poverty and a vile destitution
which they believe natural, inevitable, life in the
real. I have heard scores and scores of working
people speak about the upper classes as people
who are unreal, a nursery of children playing
with dolls'-houses. The real life is the hard
life of poverty.

"They were very warm to me," says the
Plumber. "I tell you it was no fun to have a
two-foot steel rule walking round your ribs.
Anything not done just as they wanted it to be
done, anything blundered over in the very slightest—swish!—down came the rule, and it was hell
for days afterwards. I've seen men in these
shops take up a pot of hot metal—solder—and
sling it at the head of a boy that had done something a bit cock-eye, or given a back answer. We
had to look pretty slippy, I can tell you."

Such was the hard and brutalizing start at his
trade experienced by the Plumber. But he was
quick in the uptake, his eyes were sharp with the
cunning of their childhood, he learned quickly,
did well, and had that in his nature which made
him less objectionable in the eyes of his masters
than some others—he was cheerful, amusing,
wicked. There was no occasion in his case to
teach the drink habit. Some apprentices have
to be forced to the pot. He loved it. He loved

it, perhaps, as much for its swaggering manhood as anything else, but still he loved it for itself. He got a feeling of comfort from it, and a touch of daring which exhilarated his spirits. He was quite a hard drinker all through the days of his apprenticeship. He was often manfully drunk, early in his teens, to the great delight of the plumbers.

"Up to sixteen years of age," he said, " I would pinch anything, and it all went in booze. After sixteen I pinched as a plumber, with discretion, and that, too, all went in booze."

About his boyhood's pinchings we need not inquire; sufficient is it that the training of his childhood ruled his mind with the idea that to steal was to be clever. He was, practically, entirely without the moral sense. His idea was to get money anyhow, and to spend it in drink. But after sixteen years of age—his apprenticeship left behind him, and his wages secured—he stole with discretion, he stole as a plumber.

There is one particular material used by plumbers which has a ready sale; it is sheet lead, or, in their parlance, "pigeon," occasionally "bluey." It is a part of a plumber's day—or shall we say it was a part of the old plumber's day?—to steal sufficient sheet lead to pay for the night's beer, and a bit over. No man was called a plumber who could not "carry the pin," or "carry the pony"; that is to say, who could not carry a good part of a hundredweight of sheet lead inside his trousers, suspended from a belt round his middle. This was no easy task. To steal the "bluey" was not always easy, to store it quickly away was sometimes a job, but to carry it undetected, to walk and work without crying out when the sheet slipped—this was heroic work. The Plumber at sixteen years of age proved himself a hero at this work.

To give you some idea of the extent to which this thieving is practised, let me narrate a single instance. A branch office of a well-known bank was erected near Hyde Park, and my Plumber was one of the many expert thieves employed on the job. Detectives were engaged to stand in the street, not only to watch the men at work, but to follow any of them who walked home in a manner that aroused suspicion. Now, in the contract there was an item of seven tons of sheet lead for the roof. In spite of foremen, detectives, and extra precautions in every way, only two and a half tons were used, and not a single man was caught.

Many a time my Plumber came down the long ladders with three-quarters of a hundredweight of sheet lead under his trousers' belt, and walked to his public-house, pipe in mouth, bag over his shoulder, like an honest British working-man, ready to floor any detective who aspersed his honour.

This sheet lead was carried to what plumbers call " sand shops." It is a clever phrase. It signifies " shiftiness," and stands for those shops known to every plumber in the trade as places where stolen lead is bought at current market rates. Not a working plumber in London who does not know the market price of " pigeon "; it forms a topic of conversation in public-houses throughout the town. The list of " sand shops " in London would surprise the polite world.

At the first job to which the Plumber went he had an experience which gave him a " bit of a turn." It was a building ninety feet high, near the Strand. When he had climbed the ladder and reached the roof, the men employed on the job suggested that he should cry " beer-o "—pay his footing by standing a pot of beer. My man said " No," with a Cockney's indignation at being suspected of any greenness. " You won't, won't you? " " No," he shouted, " I'll see you in hell first! "

In an instant they were round him. He was pinioned, a rope was passed under his arms, and he was dropped over the side of the roof. Down he went, in sickening jerks, for thirty or forty feet, and there he hung. " Will you cry beer-o? " they shouted from the top. And at last he had to yield. On the next day that same rope snapped with a small load of sheet lead, which fell sixty feet to the pavement below.

At eighteen, in spite of frightful waste in drink, the Plumber had sufficient money and sufficient patrons—for he is a most likable and pleasant fellow—to start in a little business of his own. He was now habitually drunk. He looks back to days when, not occasionally, but as a regular thing, he was working at the top of a ninety-rung ladder which was not tied to the roof, or crossing in hob-nailed boots iron girders stretched across nothingness eighty feet and more off the ground, quite drunk.

He never went to a job at which he did not look for something besides his work; and the proceeds of this pinching always went in drink. He tells me that the contents of a plumber's bag would astonish old gentlemen interested in museums. Let us hope that to-day it would be a monstrous thing to swell the statistics of the criminal classes with the rank and file of the plumbing trade.

"One day," he says, "I was sent for to a toff's house to look for an escape of gas. Me and my mate found the escape, and it took some finding, too, for it was behind a wainscot; but while we were looking for the escape, we found something else—a box of Havannah cigars. Into my bag they went, sharp; and at that minute in comes the toff himself.

"'Well, have you found it?'

" 'Yes, sir, we've found it, sir, and a nasty one, too, sir.'

" ' Here's a shilling for yourselves, you've done well.'

" 'Yes, sir, I think we have; thank you, sir,' and we walked out, two splendid specimens of the honest British working man! But it was always like that. *And never once a feeling of shame.*"

Money easily earned, he quotes with emphatic conviction, is money easily spent, which means beer. He earned pounds every week, and sometimes on Saturday afternoon he was pawning his tools for the evening's finish-up.

" Ah," he says, " to give you an idea of the jolly friends a man gets in that way; not once, but many times, my pals have said to me, ' Put your tools up the spout, old boy, we'll see you through, we'll get 'em out for you,' and after having drunk the money away, when I came to ask them for help, ' Get 'em out yourself,' they'd answer; ' you put 'em up, you get 'em down.' Later on, when I was starving—yes, starving!— those men wouldn't give me a crust, not one of them."

He got married before he was twenty, and he vowed soon afterwards that if his baby was a boy he'd get really drunk to celebrate the event. But he was impatient, and couldn't wait. He began three months before the child was born, and for seven years after he was always profoundly drunk. He lost job after job. In two houses they found him flat on his back in the cellar with the taps of the wine-casks spurting over his face. Ferocity began to manifest itself in his temper. He was strong, and handy with his fists. He fought many a fight with the naked fists. He picked up a foreman who corrected him one day, and threw him through a glass window. He was always in trouble. His private business vanished altogether. He had to go about looking for work.

Then this man, bred from infancy to drink and to steal, uninstructed in the first letters of morality, educated only in sharpness, cunning, and clever dishonesty, but who had preserved all through this base and scurvy career the natural good-humour and cheerfulness of his temperament, became one of those wretches who play the tyrant in the house that they have ruined. The Plumber took to flogging his starved children— one of them, a little girl, said to him in my presence, looking up into his face with a cunning smile, " We've often felt the buckle-end of your belt, haven't we, daddy? "—took to flogging, kicking, and striking these poor starved children, so that at the first sound of his footsteps on the stair they would run for cover under the bedstead. His wife withstood him. He fought her. He proved himself her master. He went out from the room where she lay, beaten and half stunned, a proud man. But his wife was not cowed. She nagged him. He never came home but she reproached him for his brutality, his drunkenness, his abhorrent cruelty. One day in a fit of ungovernable rage, he seized her, flung her down the flight of stairs, raced down after her, and aimed a blow at her head, which split the top of the banister and scarred his wrist for life. He all but murdered her.

And for drink, everything he could lay his hands on was sold. The furniture went from his home, his tools, the clothes of the children— everything.

He got to the lowest depth but one to which drink can bring a man. He reached that horrible stage where his wife stands with her children at the door of a public-house waiting for the husband to come out. He spent money on beer while the children of his body starved and shivered and cried at the door. He never experienced one pang of remorse. Never once did his conscience upbraid him. He got beer by hook or by "crook"; there for him the universe ended.

One day the news reached him that his oldest mate, and the closest companion of all his early depravity, had joined the local corps of the Salvation Army. It made no difference to the Plumber. Drunk at his work, he went straight to the public-house, delivered there on occasion, for the diversion of the company, mock sermons or sang comic songs, and only went out at closing-time, followed home through the rain and the darkness and the cold by his wife with a baby at her breast.

He was in one of his favourite public-houses when his wife opened the door one day, entered, and said to him, " Come out, or give me money for the children's food."

He took no notice. She waited, looking at him—watched by the publican and the potman—and then retired to the door. The Plumber's mates began to say, " I wouldn't have the old woman follow *me* about." He lifted his face from his beer, turned his head, and shouted to the woman at the door to get out, like a dog.

She said that she should wait there till he left.

" Will you? " he cried, with an oath, laying down his pot. And in a clumsy stride or two he had delivered a running kick with his hobnail boot at the mother of his children. She moved away, and escaped a fatal injury.

He followed her to the door. " God! " he cried, " if you don't leave me alone, I'll——" He had exhausted blasphemy and menace. He paused for a moment, and concluded, " I'll sign the pledge."

" Oh, you've often done that," she retorted, " and wetted it every time! "

Now what actual spring worked in his mind

at these words it is difficult to say, difficult to conjecture. One can find nothing in the man's past to suggest a thesis. But the words of his wife produced an extraordinary effect in his mind. He did not return to the public-house; he did not go home with her; he walked away like a man in a dream. He only knows that he was impelled to walk away. As he passed the big hall occupied by the Salvation Army, he says he suddenly felt himself grow stiff through all his joints, his feet appeared to strike root into the ground, he was unable to move. There he stood, this drunk man—dazed, bewildered, quiet—like a sleep-walker.

While he stood there the thought occurred to him of his old mate who had joined the Salvation Army. Whence came this idea, he does not know; but it came. A desire to see this man made itself felt in the Plumber's heart, and with the desire the tension of his limbs relaxed. He walked forward and made his way up the stairs to the hall door. The only officers present at that time were women. When they saw this terrible drunken man approaching, they were afraid, and chained the door against him. He looked like murder.

" Don't be afraid," he said. " I only want to know where —— lives."

They told him over the chain, and he walked away.

He found his friend in his room.

" Charlie," he said, " I want to get out of what I am. Do you think I can do it? "

" Not alone," said the other.

" Tell me, for Christ's sake! "

" Do you mean it? Are you in earnest? "

" If ever I was in my life."

" Well, then, you've just got to tell God what you've told me. Do it now. Kneel down. Tell Him."

And the Plumber knelt down and uttered his first prayer.

He rose dazed, confused, shaken. He was trembling like a leaf.

The other said, " You must come to the meeting to-night, and you must go to the penitent form, and say out loud that you're sorry, that you want the new life, and that you know you can do nothing yourself to get it. How do you feel now? "

" All of a twitter," said the Plumber.

He went out into the streets alone. He was conscious of some great change in himself which seemed to affect the world outside of him. He was glad in himself, and the outside world seemed glad. The pavements shone with fire, the distance was a haze of bright light, the leaves of all the trees in the road, he says, seemed like hands waving to him. He felt that he had come out of nightmare into a dream. He was aware that

Something had gone out of him, that he had no desire for any of the things which hitherto this vanished Something had driven him to seek; he was aware of a swimming and hovering brightness inhabiting the place in his thought from which this Something had been expelled. He was so happy that he could have shouted for joy. He was so frightened of losing this ethereal happiness that he dared not think about it. The drunken man walked in a shining light on pavements of fire, with the trees waving to him, with his soul dazed by ecstasy.

That night he went to the meeting, made his public confession, and rose up with a deepened conviction that he had got a new life.

On the following morning, for the first time in his life untormented by a craving for alcohol or tobacco, he yet found himself with insufficient courage to face the service in the open-air, dreading the mockery of the world. But he went to the evening meeting, and returned home past many a public-house without the smallest desire to enter.

He went to his work next day, guessing what welcome he would receive from his mates. He spoke to no one, and went straight to the unfinished room of a great building in which his work lay, and began his job.

In a few minutes the door opened, and a group

of his old friends entered, plumbers by trade and plumbers by soul.

" Morning, Alf."

" Morning."

" Ain't you dry? "

" No."

" Ain't you got a thick head? "

" No."

" Wouldn't you like half a gauge now? "

" No."

" What, not just half a gauge to oil the works? "

" No."

After a pause, " See your friend on Saturday, Alf? "

" Yes."

" Go to the Salvation Army? "

" Yes."

" Did you find Jesus? "

" Yes."

They burst out laughing. " What! And you a mock-preacher, proving there isn't no God? Stow it, Alf! Look here, you take it quietly by yourself, when no one is looking "—and they put a bottle of beer on the floor by his feet, and went out, closing the door.

At twelve o'clock they came back. The beer was not drunk. They examined the cork. They tasted the liquor to see that water had not been put to it. Then they turned, and with filthy words, vile phrases, and horrible blasphemies assaulted the poor soul that had been born again. Brutal as they were, one must not judge them too harshly. The change was made suddenly, and only a saint really believes in repentance for sin. The best of us are suspicious of the prodigal son: we never believe that the lost sheep prefers in its heart the fold to the mountain.

For two or three days the Plumber suffered bitterly at his work. He was mocked, taunted, teased, and insulted with studied and incessant cruelty. He bore it without reproach. Before the end of the week was reached a day came for the "rhubarb," that is to say, a subsidy, or an advance of their wages. This was paid in a public-house. The Plumber went with the rest. While he waited for the foreman he was offered beer and chaffed unmercifully about salvation. When he received his money, they told him, with a savage satisfaction, that a score was against him on the slate for fifteen shillings. He paid this money—a small part of the price of his past sins—and walked out of the public-house.

He went home.

When he entered the room where his children had suffered so terribly, and where absolute starvation had only been kept at bay by the toil of his wife, he realized that this was his first home-coming as a penitent. The woman and the children knew that some change had taken place in him; the woman believed that in a drunken moment he had joined the Salvation Army. She expected that he would be drunk on the day of the " rhubarb "; none believed in the miracle.

They stood amazed, gaping at him, because he had come back straight from work. The children looked frightened, the woman dazed.

He went to his wife, and said, " You want a bit of money, I expect," and gave her a sovereign.

She stared at him, and then looked down at the gold coin in the palm of her hand. The children glanced nervously at each other, and held their breath.

There was a silence in the desolate room for a moment, the man awkward, the woman dazed, the children confounded.

At last he said, " The kids would like a bit of dinner, wouldn't they? Shall we go along and buy a piece of meat?"

She continued to look from him to the coin, from the coin to him.

" I'm ready to go, if you are," he said.

She raised her eyes to his, and studied him. " Alf," she said, " do you mean it?"

" Yes," he said, and, getting rid of nervousness, he kissed her.

It was the first time he had kissed his wife, literally, for years. It was the first time since their first baby was born that he had come home not drunk and not tyrannous. All the bitter suffering of the long past, all the cruel blows and torturing neglect, all the hunger and ache, the poverty, wretchedness, shame, and despair of her life crowded the woman's brain, and she broke down under the overpowering contrast of this new thing in her life—affection and kindness.

Was the hard past really at an end? Was the long monotony of cruelty, starvation, and despair to which she had now become habituated, truly broken?

For that day, at any rate, there was happiness in the home.

In the morning the Plumber returned to his work. He was not subjected to mockery, but he was given all the hardest and dirtiest jobs. He was so happy that he did not resent this treatment. He began to sing Salvationist hymns.

The foreman approached. " Stow that music," he said.

" Why? "

" The other men object to it, and I don't wonder, either."

The Plumber worked in silence. Presently the other men in his vicinity began to sing. They sang all the vilest songs they could think of, songs that parody pure love, religion, and even elementary refinement, with the lowest and most abominable filthiness.

The Plumber was not a man to take persecution of this kind with meekness. He went to the foreman, and said, " If I mayn't sing hymns, these chaps mustn't sing beastliness; you've stopped me, stop them."

He carried his point, and the others left him alone.

The last tyranny of fellow-workmen now fell to his experience. He was put to Coventry. No one spoke to him. Among all those men, his former mates and companions, he worked in silence and in isolation, his presence, his existence ignored by everybody, both by men and boys.

A French friend of mine said to me the other day, " I do not think the Salvation Army will ever be so great a success in France as in England; in France one is more sensitive to ridicule, more obedient to public opinion." This remark made me think of the Plumber. Consider his stubborn courage, his masculine endurance under persecution. He was one against many, in an employment which necessitated the closest companionship; and the opposing majority were men with whom he had thieved, drunk, blasphemed, and jested for many years. It must not be supposed either that he was so carried away by religious exaltation as to make tyranny a small matter to him, or that his nature was too coarse and his sensitiveness too blunt for suffering. He was a London workman making a fight for his soul. The first uprush of spiritual freedom which had swept him out of all his old habits had now departed. He was left to fight his battle with normal powers. He was an ordinary man fighting for decency, respectability and holiness, in the midst of men who knew every letter in his iniquitous and depraved past. He felt their cruelty sharply. A companionable man, fond of comic songs and hilarious bar frolic—he felt keenly this loneliness, isolation, and neglect.

For a day or two he endured the cruelty of Coventry. Then came the end of the week. He received the remainder of his wages in a public-house, and was told that the job was postponed for a week or two, and that no one would be required on the following Monday.

He went home.

It seemed to him a hard thing, just when he had made this fresh start and the desolate room was beginning to put on the appearance of a home, that the means of daily bread should be taken from him. The workman who is told on Saturday that he will not be required on Monday loses the feeling that Sunday is a day of rest; he carries home with him a load heavier than sheet lead.

The Plumber did not say anything to his wife about this end of the job. He read a little cheap New Testament which he had bought, and experienced a sense of comfort from the words, " I am the Vine, and ye are the branches." He thought

that if he trusted to Christ all would go well with
him.   The family spent a happy Sunday.   There
was food in the house, the father was sober;
there was money enough to last with care till the
next " rhubarb."

On the Monday morning he woke early, and
went out as if to go to his regular work.   When
he found himself in the street something urged
him, before looking for a job, to go to the scene
of his last employment, the place at which work
had so suddenly terminated on the Saturday.   He
was prepared for what he found there.   The
usual operations were going on, all his mates
were at work; the sound of their toil filled the
morning air.

He stood looking at the busy scene for a few
moments, listening to the familiar sounds, watch-
ing the well-known figures, and feeling in his
heart a certain bitterness which almost stirred
him to the violence of anger.   He walked away,
feeling that the hand of every man was against
him.

Here at the very outset of a new life was the
world's oppugnance.   His world would receive
him if he came drunk and disreputable; while he
remained religious and upright it closed its gates
against him.   The hatred of religion has many
forms; none is so cruel as that which takes away
the daily bread of the workman trying to be a
better man.

Now began for the Plumber a martyrdom which searched his soul. Wherever he went he found that the story of his life had preceded him. There are, apparently, few trades in London more closely knit and with ramifications more far-reaching and swift than this trade of plumbing. A story concerning the trade flies to all corners of the metropolis; a man who gives offence becomes instantly known to mates whom he has never seen and whose names he has never heard. The poor Plumber discovered, wherever he went, that no one had work for him.

Very often he felt as if his heart would break, but never once did the temptation either to drink or to smoke visit his mind. Hungry, he felt no longing for the lulling stupefaction of tobacco; dejected and in despair, he felt no craving for the oblivionizing magic of alcohol. But a deepening melancholy settled on his mind, and again and again he had to remind himself of the words, " I am the Vine, ye are the branches," to keep alive in his heart the faith that God cared.

I want to make this picture clear and vivid in the reader's mind. Many times the out-of-work Plumber rose at five o'clock in the morning, and with nothing to sustain his physical energy except a glass of water, started out to tramp all day in quest of work. These tramps carried him sometimes as far as Harrow and Watford, well outside the boundaries of London; and he went steadily forward all the long day, with no other support than his glass of cold water and his religion. Sometimes, weary and heartsick, glancing forward and behind to see that he was not observed, this poor fellow would sink on his knees in the middle of a country road, and make his prayer, " O God, don't forsake me!" And when his feet dragged and his body seemed about to collapse, he would lie down in a ditch, take his Testament from his pocket, and read some of those parables which declare that God does care, and cares greatly, for man and his sorrows. What a picture this presents to the mind! The professional tramp has put us out of sympathy with the respectable workman genuinely seeking employment; but consider this man, converted from depravity to self-respect, this poor London workman trying to be a good man, kneeling in the dust of a country road, and reading the Galilæan parables in a Buckinghamshire ditch.

The home was only kept together during these difficult months by the incessant labour of the wife. Starvation was always at the door. The man himself certainly lived in a state of starvation. And yet—how can science explain the matter?—in spite of mental misery and the terrible state of a body reduced to extreme weakness by starvation, not once did this ex-dipsomaniac feel any desire whatever either for tobacco or alcohol.

If ever a man was tempted to drink, if ever a man had justification for drinking, surely it was this poor hungry animal, tramping the roads and streets, day after day, week after week, month after month, and always in vain, seeking for work.

He tells me that he was not in the least conscious of religious exaltation. He derived comfort from singing hymns as he trudged along the road, and he was always aware of support when he repeated the words, " I am the Vine, and ye are the branches," but never did his heart sing with a great joy, never did he feel inclined to laugh at his troubles; never did ecstasy take him out of himself and make terrestrial life appear a small matter. Always he was a hungry man asking for work. He was now so devoted to the children, who had once feared him, that he could not prevent occasional bitterness at the reflection of his present lot; he wanted, God knew how he wanted, to make his home happy and bright; he would work hard from morning to night, he would save money, and never again waste a penny in drink, tobacco, gambling, and other vices; but —there was no work for him. Alas, such is the fate of thousands of good men and capable tradesmen in modern civilization.

At last he saw that he must abandon his trade and its high wages.

He might have gone to the " Starvation Army "

and got work, but something prevented him from
bringing himself to live in this manner.   Thousands and thousands of men working for the
Army never have received a penny from its
funds; they will not let their mates say that they
turned religious in order to get work; they are
very loyal to the honour of the religion which
has saved them.

This tradesman, used to high wages and interesting work, hired himself out at last as what is
called a common labourer.   He ceased to be a
plumber.   It was a hard step, but once taken he
was glad.   By hard work, careful economy, and
enthusiasm for the home, he now lives a happy
and contented life free of all regret, and only
occasionally darkened by the anxiety of penury.
He says, speaking of his home, " Pictures hang
on the walls—they used to hang on the wife's
face."   Every day his eldest little girl goes to
meet him at his work, and walks home with him;
she was one of those who rushed under the bed
for cover at the first sound of his step on the
stair.   He is a labourer, a sweeper of the London
streets, and he is happy.   The man's face is a
*Te Deum.*   His gratitude to God, his enthusiasm
for conversion, his certain conviction that it is
only religion which can reform the individual
and the State, make him a tremendous worker
among the lost and unhappy.

And it was this man—here, I think, is the

romance of religion as a force in the strange lives
of a shabby London quarter—who, coming happy
from his home for a meeting in the Salvation
Army hall—by a chance word to the Puncher,
fresh from prison, turned that remarkable man
from murder to a life of devotion and service.

What other force can society devise which will
take such a man as this Plumber, bred in drunkenness and crime, and convert him from a thief,
a dipsomaniac, and a domestic tyrant, into an
upright, honourable, and pure-minded citizen?
Conversion is quite properly a subject for psychological examination, but modern theology misses
its chief weapon against the attacks of materialism when it fails to insist upon the immense
significance of these spiritual miracles. Whatever conversion may be, whatever its physical
machinery, it is religion and only religion which
can put the machinery in motion, and make a bad
man a good man, a profitless and dangerous citizen a useful member of society. Surely this story
of the Plumber, even as it is narrated here in a
few pages of print, must bring home to the minds
of politicians and sociologists really acquainted
with the appalling condition of modern London,
that here in religion is the one great hope of
regeneration, the one certain guarantee, as the
whole of Tolstoy's work teaches, of a noble
posterity. There is really nothing else.

# RAGS AND BONES

IN some ways the man in this story is the most original and striking of the group with whom I discussed religious experience in poor London. Certainly the manner of his conversion is quite different from the usual narratives recorded in books. I can find nothing like it in *The Varieties of Religious Experience*.

Let me begin by attempting to paint his portrait. He is very like the popular idea of a burglar: his nose is brief, and flat to the face, somewhat broken; he has a long upper lip; his mouth is twisted into a snarl; his light-coloured, bird-like eyes glare fiercely at you under a heavy and overhanging forehead; the colour of the old face, which is ploughed with deep wrinkles and marked by bitter suffering, is like dirty linen— that peculiar prison-tinge, half grey, half brown, which suggests stubborn powers of resistance and the habit of silent thought. He is vigorous and powerful, with jerky movements and passionate gestures. His voice has the fog of London in its growl. When he laughs his eyes remain hard, and his mouth is like a cat's when it draws back its lips. He is impatient of subtle questions, strikes the table often with a clenched fist, occasionally yields to a kind of ecstasy in the midst of eating bread and butter—throwing back his head and shouting " Glory to God! " in the direction of the ceiling, his face wrinkled up and contorted as though he was suffering physical torture.

He has suffered; he tells you that he *knows*. He is rugged, irregular, real.

One does not quite know what to make of this rough old son of the slums, except to say that he has suffered frightfully, that he has been delivered from hopeless despair in a miraculous manner, and that he is now as firmly fixed in righteousness as any saint of mysticism. As to the mystery of his consciousness, as to his ideas of God and the nature of existence waiting humanity beyond the grave, one can conjecture nothing.

He began life in misery. He was the child of parents who spent all their money in drink. His infancy was spent in his mother's arms in the " Queen's Arms " or the "Royal Arms," a double embrace which afforded his young soul little acquaintance either with maternal affection or royal favour. His early childhood was also spent chiefly in public-houses, where he stood at his mother's knee half suffocated in a dark and moving world of trousers, petticoats, and spilt liquor. By the time he was tall enough to see the counter he was old enough to fend for himself in the streets; he preferred them to the tavern. He had long been used to going home with his mother after midnight, and now he very often waited for her outside the public-house door until he was so tired that he crawled away to sleep in a yard or a doorway. The streets had no terrors for him.

This life of neglect, misery, and destitution, by some miracle, did not depress Teddy. He grew up, in spite of it, sharp, active, acute, and humorous. He was sharp enough to provide himself with food, to avoid thrashings from his father, and to find comfortable dosses in backyards. Later, he was acute enough to see that the ranks of an infantry regiment was the best place for a hungry, growing boy. He enlisted and soldiered without distinction, but without great crime, till his time was up. Throughout his soldiering he was a cockney humorist.

Drink was getting hold of him; but he was strong, and could carry a " skinful." He came out of the army a hard drinker, but not a drunkard. He had his wits about him.

He became a marine-store dealer, that is to say, a rag-and-bone merchant in a very small way of business. His liveliness, his fondness for drink, and his endless stories of sharp practice and cunning, made him popular and brought him business. But as fast as money came in—not very fast, perhaps—he drank it away. Then he married a good woman, and his wife exercised a certain restraint over him. Things began to go better. He was really deeply attached to his wife, and for her sake he made a manful fight to keep out of the public-houses; there were whole weeks when he did not drink a glass of beer or waste a penny in the taverns. His home was really a very happy one, as happiness goes in shabby London.

But terrible disaster overtook him. His wife died. He was left quite alone in the world. It was the death of his wife which made him an habitual drunkard. Before that he had no over-mastering craving. Strong-willed and tenacious, he had power over his appetite, could control it, and make it obedient. But the death of his wife broke him down, and drove him to alcohol for consolation. One must try to understand alcohol's fatal attraction for the poor.

"The sway of alcohol over mankind," says Professor James, "is unquestionably due to its power to stimulate the mystical faculties of human nature, usually crushed to earth by the cold facts and dry criticisms of the sober hour. Sobriety diminishes, discriminates, and says no; drunkenness expands, unites, and says yes. It is, in fact, the great exciter of the *Yes* function in man. It brings its votary from the chill periphery of things to the radiant core. It makes him

for the moment one with truth. Not through
mere perversity do men run after it. To the poor
and the unlettered it stands in the place of sym-
phony concerts and of literature; and it is part
of the deeper mystery and tragedy of life that
whiffs and gleams of something that we immediately recognize as excellent should be vouch-
safed to so many of us only in the fleeting earlier
phases of what in its totality is so degrading and
poisoning. The drunken consciousness is one bit
of the mystic consciousness, and our total opinion
of it must find its place in our opinion of that
larger whole.

" Nitrous oxide and ether, especially nitrous
oxide, when sufficiently diluted with air, stimulate
the mystical consciousness in an extraordinary
degree. Depth beyond depth of truth seems revealed to the inhaler. This truth fades out, however, or escapes, at the moment of coming to;
and if any words remain over in which it seemed
to clothe itself, they prove to be the veriest non-
sense. Nevertheless, the sense of a profound
meaning having been there persists; and I know
more than one person who is persuaded that in
the nitrous oxide trance we have a genuine meta-
physical revelation. Some years ago I myself
made some observations on this aspect of nitrous
oxide intoxication, and reported them in print.
One conclusion was forced upon my mind at that
time, and my impression of its truth has ever

since remained unshaken. It is that our normal
waking consciousness, rational consciousness, as
we call it, is but one special type of consciousness,
whilst all about it, parted from it by the filmiest
of screens, there lie potential forms of consciousness entirely different. We may go through life
without suspecting their existence, but apply the
requisite stimulus, and at a touch they are there
in all their completeness, definite types of men-
tality which probably somewhere have their field
of application and adaptation. No account of the
universe in its totality can be final which leaves
these other forms of consciousness quite disre-
garded."

This is so true that one surely need not em-
phasize it; but, unfortunately, too many who
strive to cure people of alcoholism will not recognize that they are endeavouring to take away a
man's escape from misery, his one means of
flight into the rapturous air of illusion; they per-
sist in treating drunkenness as a form of greedi-
ness quite similar to a schoolboy's stomach-ache
from overbunning; in this way they fail in their
good intentions.

The psychological aspect of alcoholism is one
that opens the door to much mystery, and reveals
to those who look long enough and deep enough
puzzling glimpses of the human soul.

This rough man, an ex-soldier and now a rag-
and-bone merchant, finding himself bowed down

by the death of a woman he had loved sincerely
and nobly, went to drink for oblivion, stood in
a public-house to forget the grave, laughed with
the drinkers to forget his desolate home, drank
and drank to stop the bleeding of his heart. And
he discovered happiness. The filmy screens surrounding his normal consciousness lifted with the
potent fumes, and he inhabited fields of consciousness wide, glorious, and delightful. It is important to know that he became a happy drunkard. Some men find in alcohol a deadening and
soporific narcotic; they grow sullen, silent, quarrelsome in a grumbling, growling way; others,
and of this company was our poor widower,
discover in alcohol a Jinni, or, if you like, an
Ifrit, who lifts them up to the seventh heaven,
transports them over stellar spaces, builds for
them in the twinkling of an eye palaces of por-
phyry and jasper, fills their hands with gold, and
breathes into their souls the sense and the conviction of absolute power. From deep melancholy this man rose to dazzling heights of happiness. Alcohol, like the magic carpet, lifted
him into mid-air; like the ivory-tube, revealed
to him all he desired to see; like the enchanted
apple, healed him of all sickness.

Because he was so intensely happy, he became
immensely popular. The wretched Miserables
who congregated in his public-houses for happiness and oblivion, welcomed his company, laughed

at his jests, applauded his songs, loved him in their drunken sodden joy for the wonderful contagion of his joviality.

For a long time, for years, this state of things continued.

Then his business dwindled and failed. He was in trouble for his rent. Sharper men served his customers. He went laughing and singing to his ruin, caring not a jot what became of him. So long as he had the magic of alcohol, what mattered rags and bones?

He took to sleeping in yards, in dustbins, in any dog-hole or cellar that he could stumble into unobserved by midnight police.

He got his living—that is to say, money for drink—by a hundred clever dodges. Although this man has a face which reminds one of Flaxman's fiends, throughout his life he has been inoffensive, always he has enjoyed popularity. " No one can help liking old Teddy " is a phrase in the district. The man is reckoned clever. He would take the laces out of his boots, go into public-houses where he was not known, and offer them for sale. He made money in this fashion, and could sleep with the laces in his pocket, ready for the next day's traffic. His eyes were keen to notice vendible things in backyards and in gutters. He cadged his way through life, without committing crimes. In a moment of destitution he got hold of a sheet of newspaper,

tore it into strips, and sold them at a penny each
as "bringers of luck." He was too good-tem-
pered to be a criminal.

But he found it harder and ever harder to pick
up sufficient money to satisfy his increasing craving for drink. He sank deeper into the gutter,
his joviality began to leave him, his old companions showed less disposition to pay for his
drink, less disposition to listen to his jests. For
one thing, his clothes were now the foul rags of
a tramp. Alcohol is an Ifrit that has the habit
of leaving its victims at an awkward moment.
The magic worlds fade away. The palaces dis-
solve and melt. Consciousness narrows to a pint
pot.

Once at this point in his career he had what is
called "a turn." After having slept in various
areas and certain conveniences attached to public-
houses for a long period, he discovered an old
muddy, broken-down cart in a yard, which was
never disturbed by its owner, and which offered
shelter from wind and rain. Here he established
himself, and this old cart became his home.
People got to know about it. They laughed at
Teddy's "doss." He slunk into the yard at one
or two in the morning, climbed into the cart,
lay in his rags on the floor, and slept soundly
till the dawn.

Well, one cold night after a fairly successful
day, he found himself with coppers enough for a

" fourpenny kip "—that is to say, a bed in a common lodging-house. Every now and then he indulged himself in this luxury, especially on occasions when whisky had excited his feelings, and his soul became princely. On this particular night he walked proudly towards his lodging-house, thinking of the kitchen fire in the basement, and anticipating joy from a dirty sheet, a foul blanket, and a palliasse such as you would not give to your dog.

On his way he met an old tramp, a poor broken wretch known in the neighbourhood as Old Bumps. This man whined about the bitter cold, said he felt bad, wished to God he had some place where he could sleep. Teddy told him of the cart, and gave him permission to use it for that night only.

After glorious repose in the lodging-house, Teddy rose and came out into the world with renewed hope. As he walked someone met him, started, turned quite grey, and stood. " What's the matter? " asked Teddy. " Why! " cried the man, with an oath, " you're dead! " " Dead! what do you mean? " " D'you mean to tell me you're alive? " Teddy demanded explanations. " Everybody in the place is saying you're dead," replied the man; " hundreds say they have seen your corpse. You died last night in the cart. I saw them wheeling your body away."

Old Bumps had died in his sleep. Someone

had seen the body lying there. A policeman had been told. The crowd saw a corpse taken out of the cart and wheeled away in an ambulance to the mortuary. The whole world said, " Teddy is dead."

The thought that he had been considered dead had an explosive effect in Teddy's mind. It was a catherine-wheel of alarm, scattering sparks and confusion. It pulled him up. It made him reflect on death. He considered within himself that the hour surely cometh, and for him might come suddenly and soon, when a man's soul passes out of the body, and must give account of the deeds done in the body. He saw how very easily the corpse of Old Bumps might have been his corpse. He might die one night in his sleep. He might be taken out of that cart, cold, stiff, motionless. People would say, " Teddy is dead —dead like a dog!" But what of his soul?

" ' Love would not be love,' says Bourget, ' unless it could carry one to crime.' And so one may say that no passion would be a veritable passion unless it could carry one to crime." (Sighele, *Psychologie des Sectes,* p. 136.)

On this Professor James comments, " In other words, great passions annul the ordinary inhibitions set by ' conscience.' And conversely, of all the criminal human beings, the false, cowardly, sensual, or cruel persons who actually live, there is perhaps not one whose criminal impulse may

not be at some moment overpowered by the presence of some other emotion to which his character
is also potentially liable, provided that other emotion be only made intense enough. Fear is usually the most available emotion for this result in
this particular class of persons. It stands for
conscience, and may here be classed appropriately
as a ' higher affection.' If we are soon to die,
or if we believe a day of judgment to be near
at hand, how quickly do we put our moral house
in order—we do not see how sin can evermore
exert temptation over us! Old-fashioned hell-
fire Christianity well knew how to extract from
fear its full equivalent in the way of fruits for
repentance, and its full conversion value."

The most available emotion—fear—began to
work in the mind of this London Miserable. He
thought, What can I do? It seemed to him that
he must first of all escape from the present life.
He could never more sleep in that cart. He must
avoid his old haunts. Best of all, he must leave
London behind him. Somewhere he must find
work. Somehow he must begin again.

So the frightened drunkard, born and bred in
the gutters of the slums, took to the road in
middle age, and tramped out of London to save
his soul.

I have never seen man's face express more
suffering than the battered, weather-beaten face
of this rag-and-bone merchant when he described

to me the horrors of a tramp's life. To tramp till the legs are like boards, the feet like burning coals, the empty stomach ravenous and tigerish for food, and everywhere to find the doors of homes shut against one, to receive only fierce or mocking looks from men, frightened or contemptuous glances from women and children; to walk on and on under a burning sky, through a downpour of rushing rain, in snow and hail, in drenching mist and blood-congealing cold— always regarded with suspicion, barked at by the dogs in farmyards and stables, followed threateningly by the village policeman, refused not only one helpful word or one kindly gift, but refused work of any kind, the hardest and most menial— this is an experience which hardens a man's heart, turns the blood to vinegar, and makes him the savage enemy of his own kind.

Nor was it much better when he reached the shelter of a workhouse. No effort was made to save his soul, to humanize his heart with kindness. No one ever sought to reclaim him, to provide him with manly work, to hold out the hope of wages, home, and self-respect. From the moment when the door of the workhouse opened he was treated as a criminal. Hard words and hard looks accompanied him to his bed, and before he could eat a workhouse breakfast he had to break—this broken tramp, starving for nourishment—half a ton of stones. Many a time

on the road he felt deserted by man and God, and
driven by some inexorable devil onwards to
greater suffering and more terrible hell.  Again
and again he abandoned hope, lived in blackest
despair, and only refrained from self-destruction
out of fear of hell.  And all the time he was
tortured by a craving for alcohol, which was like
a fire burning at his vitals.

He told me a curious story.  He had tramped
one day across Salisbury Plain, and on the point
of collapse from starvation, he sank down in a
ditch, and covering his face with his hands,
weeping like a child, he cried aloud, " O God, give
me something to eat! "  A feeling of help came
to him in the midst of his exhaustion and despair.
He took his hands from his face and looked to
right and left of him; not a soul was to be seen.
His eyes looked ahead of him.  In the opposite
hedge he saw a piece of paper.  He got up, convinced that there was the help he sought.  The
paper turned out to be a bag.  It contained two
scones.

A curious coincidence.

He tramped back to London, feeling that those
who knew him would be more likely to help him
than peasants and farmers who took him for a
criminal.  He arrived in his old slum such a pitiable object—" lousy as a cuckoo," in the local
phrase—that everybody turned their backs upon
him.  Here and there he managed to cadge a

drink. Now and again he picked something up in the gutters which he was able to sell for beer. Occasionally he got a copper for holding a horse. Once or twice he held the spirited cob of the Puncher, while that flash prize-fighter was drinking in saloon bars. In this manner he existed for months and months, always starving, frequently half drunk, and getting every day more dreadful a creature to look at, so that even many in like case with himself gave him a wide berth.

One day, when he was quite penniless, the craving for alcohol became so forceful and irresistible that he knew, whatever the cost, he must obtain it. At that moment he was on the edge of crime. Like a ravenous beast he went slouching at a half-run through the streets, looking with his ferocious eyes for some chance of getting money and drink. As luck would have it, he saw the landlord of a public-house in which he had spent hundreds of pounds talking to a man at the door. Teddy, in his vile rags, went up to him, and said, " Will you trust me with a pot till to-morrow? "

The landlord looked at him with contempt, and answered, " Don't you see I'm talking to a gentleman? "

But Teddy's craving was proof against insult and contempt.

" Trust me till to-morrow," he said. " I'm perishing for a drink."

The landlord made no answer.

Again Teddy made his request. This time he was told to go to hell.

" Come on," pleaded the poor wretch, " give us one chance; just a drink, only one; I'll go away quiet, if you will."

" Oh, go and mess the Army about! " said the publican, with impatient contempt.

There was a Salvation Army open-air meeting in the next street, and the sound of the band came to their ears.

" Do you mean it?—you won't? " demanded Teddy.

" Yes. You go and mess the Army about," repeated the publican. Now it must be told, what perhaps is not widely known, that in these destitute quarters of London, the publicans very often support the Salvation Army with subscriptions, and frequently encourage them to get hold of the worst drunkards. A Salvationist can always go freely into the public bar of these gin-palaces. As one of them explained to me, " A publican doesn't make anything out of a four-ale man, and when they get badly and habitually drunk, he's never over pleased to see them, for often it means a row in the bar and trouble with the police. What the publican likes is the toff, who cracks down a bob for three or four pennorth of whisky and a tuppeny smoke. There's profit there. And the toff drinks, lights his cigar, and goes—making room for others. But the four-ale man spends his twopence, and sits solid for hours, hoping to cadge another drink from some mate who never appears. Yes, the publicans support us. It pays them."

So it will be seen that this particular publican really meant it when he told Teddy to go and mess the Army about. He had no desire, perhaps, for the salvation of Teddy's soul, but he did not want him for a customer, which—from the publican's point of view—comes to the same thing.

The contempt in the words stung Teddy. He considered how much wealth he had poured into that public-house. And now, when he was mad for just one drink, just because he was penniless and in rags, the devil he had enriched ordered him, like a dog, to get out of his way. The words "go and mess the Army about" stuck in his mind. Suddenly it occurred to him that this thing called the Salvation Army was *kind* even to tramps in a condition as vile as his. It was like light to his soul. Denied by the publican, this sinner thought of Christ. There on the slum pavement, outside a tavern, mad for drink, and sunken to the very depths of misery, all of a sudden the consciousness of the outcast received the idea of Christ's kindness to the lost.

As I said at the beginning of the story, I know nothing like it in the chronicles of conversion. How different from the ecstatic vision of the mystic, how different from the glowing light suddenly suffusing the prayerful soul of the penitent, how different from the mysterious voice calling a dejected spirit to the love of God! And yet how natural, how real, how simple, in its abnormality. Also, how true to the slums!

" Right, guv'nor," said Teddy, and he said it savagely, not at all in the tone of penitence, " I'll take your tip! " and he walked away in his filth and his rags.

He went straight to the open-air meeting in the next street. The band was getting ready for the march back to the hall. Teddy approached the drummer and said, " Can I come along with you? " The drummer looked at him and said, " Yes." Teddy marched beside that man to the hall, the rattle of the drum and the blare of the trumpets making strange music in his soul. At the meeting in the hall he broke down, covered with remorse for his past life, and feeling how greatly he had rejected the mercy of God. He went to the penitent form, knelt down, and prayed with anguish for forgiveness, and also for strength to make a fresh start. " Oh, God, oh, God," he kept crying, " I want to be born again! "

He says the answer came with the cry. Then and there he felt his breast broadened, his soul lightened, and the blood coursing joyfully through his veins. He was saved.

Remember that ten minutes before this man

had been running through the streets, mad for alcohol.

The Salvationists showed him love and kindness. He was in a terrible state, one of the dirtiest men ever handled by that corps. He had no socks and no shirt. Next to the blackened flesh of his feet was the broken leather of his foul boots; next to the skin and bones of his legs, trousers that were rent and threadbare and unspeakable; next to the poor body, something that called itself a coat and was not. This man had neither socks, nor shirt, nor waistcoat; the state of his skin must not be described; they had to get an old sack to put over him. It was the case of his trade—rags and bones.

To such a condition can a man come in our modern days. To such a condition can drink bring him; to such a condition the State allows him to come. Religion took this man and saved him from the publican and the State.

Here, you may be tempted to think, is the case of a man merely saved by being provided with work; a man who made use of religion to obtain employment, and lived his repentance more or less comfortably on the wages of charity.

Hear the end.

He left the hall, after his conversion, and without saying a word to any of his friends, walked about the streets for two nights. As a rule the Army carefully looks after its penitents, but in

Teddy's case there was an accident. Everybody thought that somebody else was nursing him; in fact, no one did. They set him on a white horse next day, and led him in triumph through his old haunts, through the foulest quarters of the town, exhibiting Teddy as a converted sinner, and making a vast impression. But this Man on the White Horse was starving, and he said nothing. He never complained, he never hinted for bread or penny. He endured the agony of starvation in a noble silence. All that time he was praying a single prayer, " Oh, God! give me one chance, and I'll serve You all the days of my life." He was determined not to live by the Salvation Army—like almost all the men I talked to, he glories in the sneering title of " Starvation Army "—he was determined to provide for himself. " I didn't go to the Army for beer, nor yet for charity, nor yet for work," he cries fiercely; " that's what a good many do go for, and they go away disappointed, calling it Starvation Army. Glory to that title! The Army isn't for mouchers and work-shys, and willing-to-work-but-wonts. No; it's for those who seek Almighty God, who go on their knees to Him, and who get up with something inside them that won't ever let them cadge or whine or play the loafer again. And that's what I got. Praise God! He lifted me up from a cadging, drunken beast, and gave me a soul to praise Him and love Him

and stand firm.   Do you know how I made my
start?   I'll tell you.   It began like this.   Somebody gave me twopence.   It was my first capital.
I bought for that sum a couple of little flour
bags.   I picked them to pieces, sewed them up
again as aprons, and sold them for twopence each.
That was my start—turning twopence into fourpence.   With that fourpence I bought more flour
bags.   With every penny I made I bought something else, and sold again, till my capital was
half a crown—all made in one long day.   I was
now a man of business.   I worked like this for
weeks, till I was fairly floated; then I slept in
a Rowton House like a gentleman; I started
a rag-and-bone round, kept myself steady; saved
money, took a house, and began to do well.
Never a farthing did I take from the Army."

And now for a confession.

Some months after this amazing regeneration
the news came, " Teddy's broke it! "—which
meant Teddy had gone back to drink.   This
rumour reached the ears of the " angel-adjutant "
—it was Teddy, by the way, who gave her that
name.   The adjutant was returning home after
an exhaustive day's work, and she had a meeting
in the evening.   But the news was serious.
" Teddy's broke it! "—it meant ruin for poor
Teddy's soul.   The Man had fallen from the
White Horse.   She jumped upon her bicycle,
went to her officers, and in a few minutes the

whole corps was beating the district for this fallen star, this lost sheep, this poor dog returned to its vomit. To this day the corps sometimes speaks of the great bicycle hunt for Teddy.

They found him at last in a public-house, mad drunk. They got him back to his nice home, which they found wrecked and broken and defiled, and put him to bed.

When he came to himself he found that someone had lit a fire and had set a kettle to boil for tea, and was kneeling in the little chamber praying and crying. It was the adjutant.

The loving gentleness broke his heart.

How did he fall? He himself says now that he is all the better for that fall, that before it he was "too self-confident," not meek enough to know his own weakness, and not sensible enough to realize that only God can save a drunkard. But there was a very human disposing cause. Consider this little narrative of a fragment of London's social world: Teddy had a mother who was in the workhouse, well cared for and protected from drink by wholesome regulations. Every Sunday after his conversion he went to the workhouse, brought his mother home, gave her a shilling and a good tea, and afterwards took her safely back. But this filial affection was not good enough for the neighbours. Tongues wagged. "Everybody knew what he *should* have done!" says one of his friends contemptuously.

Well, these gossiping neighbours used to talk to Teddy's mother, get her alone and tell her she ought to make him remove her from the work-house and let her live like a lady. They worked upon her feelings, till she grew to hate her son, till she felt that it was he who put her in the House and kept her there. Then one Sunday, during his absence at the Salvation Army meeting, having filled the old woman with drink, the neighbours assisted her to smash up the home he had got together with such great labour, self-denial, and pardonable pride; they smashed up his home—to teach him filial affection.

The blow was too much for Teddy. He went out from the ruin of his house savage and disheartened, and—broke it.

The tender-heartedness of the adjutant brought him once more to the penitent form and to Christ, where this rough, big, powerful, burglar-looking man sobbed and cried like a child. And something of great importance came of this fall. While he was mad drunk in the public-house a Salvation lass had entered and commanded the publican not to serve him with any more drink. Teddy was struck by that woman, and considered her. He had prayed for a wife for his home, and now that it was ruined he felt that only a wife could help him to restore it. He made sure of the power of this second conversion, and then offered himself to the Salvationist.

She liked him—even in his drunkenness, as we
have said, everybody liked Teddy—and when
he told her all the ache and longing of his heart,
she got after a time to love him. With her love
to assist him he prospered more and more at his
business, and now, with a child in his home, the
delight of his eyes, he has one of the best rag-
and-bone rounds in aristocratic London, and his
happy home, his prosperous domesticity set an
example to his neighbours.

One day he came to the adjutant and sub-
scribed ten shillings to the funds of the local
corps. She did not like to take it, but he insisted. " They tell me," he said, " you are wor-
ried for the gas-bill." Then he said, " How much
is it, and how much have you got? " " With
your ten shillings, Teddy," she answered, " I
have got a pound, and the bill is for fifty shillings." " Thirty bob short," he said. " How long
have you got? " " Till to-morrow morning."

At eight o'clock next morning Teddy came with
the thirty shillings.

What a revolution in personality! Does one
exaggerate to call it a new birth?

## X

# APPARENT FAILURE

THIS is a strange love story. It has the interest of presenting to the reader a poor man's version of the marriage problem, a theme usually restricted by fashionable novelists to the lucky classes. Also, it has the particular interest of showing religion disappointed of a soul and yet undefeated in its tremendous conflict with evil.

When I was gathering the materials for this book, and returning every now and then for fresh air from the slums to happier places in society, I found that almost everybody to whom I spoke of my investigations said in the modern tired way, " But do these conversions last? Are they not merely disturbances of the emotions, and quite transitory in their effects?

The reader who has followed these stories with intelligence and with knowledge of human nature deeper than that which serves the average poor man-of-the-world in his journeys round the sun, will understand how I must have felt, listening to such chilling commentaries on stories like the Puncher's, the Criminal's, and the Lowest of the Low. It was not until I heard the story which now follows, the story which I have purposely reserved for the end of my book, and which I name " Apparent Failure " with a good reason, that I learned how best to silence the lounging critics of conversion—those innumerable people too shallow, I fear, to study such a work as Professor James's *Varieties of Religious Experience,* and certainly too superficial ever to experience in themselves profound spiritual changes or, indeed, any emotion of a penetrating nature.

The answer to these people is the Seventy-Times-Seven of forgiveness. Even if every person in the world, converted from infamy to purity, from crime to virtue, from selfishness to unselfishness, from cruelty to love, from hell to heaven—even if every one of them reverted to their past, still conversion would remain the sovereign force and glory of religion. For, during the period of their conversion, however brief, the lost would have been saved, hell empty, and heaven glad; during that period, however brief, sins which might have been committed remained for ever uncommitted; and during that period—how brief or how long does not matter—these people proved what the enemies of religion will not believe, with all the history of religious experience against them—that the very lowest and vilest of men are capable of noble thoughts and lives of pure unselfishness, can, over and over

again, disprove all the pessimism of " heredity "
and " environment."

And above all other considerations, this: A
man once converted, or half converted, remains
to the end of his days haunted by the pure
memory in his life, that pure interlude when hell
receded and heaven came close about his ways.
I do not believe he ever becomes wholly bad. I
think he is always more conscious of a spiritual
destiny than he was before the hour of his.half-
conversion. And from all I can gather, the man
whose half-conversion ends in apparent failure,
becomes, in his fall, little worse than most of us
who languidly commit our sins, languidly fight
against them and believe all the time that we are
worthy of the tremendous things uttered by poets
and prophets concerning man's immortal soul.

> Je suis le champ vil des sublimes combats
> Tantot l'homme d'en haut et tantot l'homme d'en bas;
> Et le mal dans ma bouche avec le bien alterne,
> Comme dans le desert le sable et la citerne.

These fallen converts, I mean, remain fighters.
They may give up religion, but they maintain
some kind of conflict with their lower natures.
Their lapse is a sin at which we must not sneer,
but which we must forgive, even with seventy-
times-seven. I would ask the reader, who doubts
the lastingness of conversion, who is prejudiced
against this pre-eminent miracle of the religious

life by the cant of a wholly bastard Christianity, and who thinks that humanity could get along very well without any religion at all, particularly emotional religion, to consider that the stories in this book are really true stories, that they represent the actual truth of poor life in London, and to reflect that they reveal, even among the most brutal, sunken, and degraded, a craving after religious satisfactions, the denial of which would impoverish their lives and make them enemies of society. To welcome the conversion of these men is to help them and to help humanity; to forgive them and bid them strive again, even if they fall headlong back to former ruin, is Christ-like; to shrug the shoulder at them, to deny the efficacy of their regeneration, is to deny the chief insisted revelation which the Founder of Christianity announced to mankind. I believe that none of these men whose stories I have tried to tell, many of them converted for a long period of years, will ever revert; but if they should relapse, all of them, I should still insist upon their temporary salvation as an argument in favour of the truth of religion, and as an argument in favour of religion as the supreme force in social regeneration.

But here follows a story of failure, apparent failure; and this story, I think, will, perhaps, more convince sceptical readers of the reality and value of conversion than any of those which have preceded it, where no question of failure arose. Also, I trust that it will create deeper sympathy for that particular religious organization whose work among the outcasts I have followed in this book, and make its methods more respected and admired by those who judge it without knowledge.

The "angel-adjutant," whose work made so great a change in the quarter of London we have glanced at in these pages, went from London to a large manufacturing town, where drink had created courts and slums almost as vile as any in the metropolis. She found that the corps of the Salvation Army to which she was now attached had many of the characteristics of a respectable and successful sect. The large hall was always more or less filled at the evening meetings, and by people who appeared to be prosperous, happy, and comfortable. In vain did she look for the Miserables, with broken heads and drunken faces, who had filled the back benches in London. She began to feel half afraid—such is the character of religious zeal—that the town was without outcasts.

But when she questioned her associates, she found that the place had Miserables enough and to spare; that there were many black slums, and that crime flourished particularly in one bad street where no one dared to breathe the name of religion. In a few days the adjutant had visited this bad street, and had laid her plans for battle.

There was one man in this quarter of the town, she discovered, who exercised more influence on the wicked than any other. He was not a criminal. He was not wholly vicious. But there was some spell of personality about him which made him a force, some strength of individuality and some charm of being, which gave him power. He was young. He was strong. Few men dared to face him in fight. His bad habit was drink.

This man was married, and lived with his mother in a common lodging-house, where he ruled the unruly and kept order in vigorous fashion; drunk or sober, this man knew the etiquette of the lodging-house and saw that it was observed. His mother was glad of him, but wished that he did useful money-earning work in the day, instead of drinking himself mad in the public-houses. Otherwise, a good son.

The adjutant perceived that if she could get this man, she would certainly draw a great many after him. She therefore concentrated her efforts on securing his sympathy.

He was astonished when this meek little woman in the poke bonnet waylaid him in the midst of that bad street, so astonished that he stood still and stared at her.

Throughout London, and, indeed, in almost all the great towns, these officers of the Salvation

Army, both men and women, are familiar figures in the worst and most dangerous streets. Desperate men and abandoned women have these people in their midst, and do them no harm, offer them no insult. As the drunken man mentioned in a footnote on another page said to this very adjutant, "never hurt the likes of you, because you care for the likes of us."

But it happened that in this particular town the bad street had not been visited even by Salvationists. The degraded people on the pavements and in the road, outside public-houses, and on the doorsteps of lodging-houses, stared at the Salvationist who confronted their terror and smiled in his face.

The terror himself was so taken aback that he listened.

The strategy of the adjutant took this form: she said that she was organizing a great meeting for the reclamation of drunkards and outcasts, that she was new to the town, and that those who knew it well warned her of opposition, and even of a riot at her meeting. And she concluded by saying that she had heard of this man's great strength and his powerful influence over others, and therefore had she come to him for protection. " I am rather afraid," she said.

He began to understand, began to be flattered.

She then asked him directly if he would come to the meeting, and if he would use his influence there to prevent lawlessness and disorder. " I am afraid—will *you* help me? "

The sweet face of this good woman, the confidence of her appeal, perhaps the gentleness of her voice, had an immediate effect upon this dangerous man. They roused in him all that was chivalrous and good and knightly. He became, even there in the street, and at this the very first appeal to his goodness, a different man. The adjutant had reached to some dim and mysterious field of consciousness. She had touched his soul.

" The great thing," says Professor James, " which the higher excitabilities give is *courage;* and the addition and subtraction of a certain amount of this quality makes a different man, a different life. Various excitements let the courage loose. Trustful hope will do it; inspiring example will do it; love will do it; wrath will do it. In some people it is natively so high that the mere touch of danger does it, though danger is for most men the great inhibitor of action. ' Love of adventure ' becomes, in such persons, a ruling passion. ' I believe,' says General Skobeleff, ' that my bravery is simply the passion, and at the same time the contempt, of danger. The risk of life fills me with an exaggerated rapture. The fewer there are to share it, the more I like it. The participation of my body in the event is required to furnish me an adequate excitement.

Everything intellectual appears to me to be reflex; but a meeting of man to man, a duel, a danger into which I can throw myself headforemost, attracts me, moves me, intoxicates me. I am crazy for it, I love it, I adore it. I run after danger as one runs after women; I wish it never to stop. Were it always the same, it would always bring me a new pleasure. When I throw myself into an adventure in which I hope to find it, my heart palpitates with the uncertainty; I could wish at once to have it appear and yet to delay. A sort of painful and delicious shiver shakes me, my entire nature runs to meet the peril with an impetus that my will would in vain try to resist.' "

Such a man, with the difference made by nationality, education, and social environment, was this terror of the bad street to whom our adjutant made her appeal. It was his courage, his love of danger, which made him respond to her petition with a vigorous promise to see her through with her meeting.

That meeting filled the great hall to overflowing with the worst people in the town. The announcement that certain well-known former bad characters would speak, testify to conversion, attracted the crowd; and the rumour that Jack, their own local terror, was to be among the audience roused a widespreading curiosity.

For the first time the new hall was literally

filled with those people to whom the Salvation
Army makes it a most earnest part of their mission to minister—the vile, the degraded, the abandoned, and the lost, those off-scourings of our
nation almost entirely neglected by all other religious bodies.    Jack kept order with a bullying
energy till the meeting began, warning the mockers and the drunken that he would pitch them
out and give them rough handling if they disturbed the little woman's entertainment.

They sang a hymn to begin with, then there
was a prayer, then the adjutant read her favourite
parable of the Prodigal Son.    So far there was
no disorder, and Jack's duties carried him no
further than scowling in the direction of those
he wanted to fall upon and chastise, but who,
vexatiously enough, behaved with every possible
propriety.

Then followed the testimonies.

Jack soon forgot to look about for disorder.
He stood in the front of the standing pack which
occupied the back of the hall listening.  He saw
men who had been prize-fighters, criminals,
tramps, and petty thieves standing clean and
happy on the platform speaking of the joy that
had come to them with conversion, and explaining
that conversion meant a surrender of man's mutinous will to the will of a God all-anxious to care
for them.    Again and again came the assurance:
" However bad any man here may feel himself

to be, however hopeless and ashamed and lost
he may feel, he has only to come out publicly
to this penitent form, kneel down and ask God
for His mercy, to have the load lifted off his soul
and to feel himself strong in the strength of
Almighty God to overcome all his temptations."

When, at the end of the meeting, the formal
invitation was made, among the many wretched
and miserable souls who advanced to the form
was this local terror who had come to keep
order.

The same spirit which had impelled him to
come to the meeting impelled him to the form.
He was brought to see that, with all his strength
and courage, drink was his master and he its
slave.  His honour was touched.  To make a
fight against such a tyrant struck him as a grand
conflict, one of Victor Hugo's *" sublimes com-
bats."*  He rose up and went to the form, because it was a difficult thing to do, because
it required courage.  He was not drawn there,
touched by compassion for the Man of Sorrows
or ecstasied by love of God; he was not, perhaps,
in any mood of imaginable repentance.  All the
changes in his brain ran into the one channel
of energy: " I am not afraid; I will do this thing;
I will get the Victory."

When the adjutant told me of this meeting, she
said: " Jack was converted from drink, but that
is not the real thing."

Nevertheless, it was a very great thing. He rose up from his knees a changed and altered man. He said he was saved—meaning that he felt conscious of profound change in his spiritual being. He said he would come regularly to the meetings, and promised to bring others with him. He went out happy and confident.

Now, there was tragedy in this man's life. He had married in his youth a woman who had neither the power to keep him good nor the ability to resist in herself the contagion of his example. She had come to a state of moral feebleness which inspired in her husband nothing but disgust. He had thrashed her cruelly on many occasions, without altering her character; he now appealed to her from his vantage of respectability, equally in vain. She sank lower and lower.

To the man making his fight against drink the companionship of this poor creature was odious and sometimes maddening.

The adjutant saw how things were, tried to save the woman, tried to make the man patient under his provocation, and watched over that interesting drama with anxiety and solicitude. One day it reached her that the man had fallen back into drunkenness.

She got upon her bicycle and rode immediately to the bad street. She was half-way down the evil road when she saw him. He was in the midst of a bloody fight with his brother. Like two madmen, their faces horrible with cuts, bruises, and blood, the two men rushed and struck at each other with all the passion of murder. To interfere with those madmen seemed like madness. But the adjutant got off her bicycle, gave it to one of the crowd, and going in amongst the fighters, caught hold of her man and implored him to desist. He shook her off with a foul oath, warning her that he would strike her if she interfered, and rushed upon his brother again with added hate and new fury. There was a stable close by, with the door open. It flashed through the adjutant's brain that the crowd in the street kept up the excitement of the fight. She waited till the brothers were locked together close to this open door, and then—how she did it she does not know—she threw herself upon them both, pushed them into the stable, shut the door in a flash and locked it.

Bruised and terribly wounded, the lapsed convert came to the next meeting, knelt afresh at the penitent form, and vowed that he would never again give way to drink.

The adjutant saw what fine courage this man possessed to come publicly in his shame, under the watchful eyes of his bad neighbourhood, once again to implore the forgiveness and help of God. But she feared that conversion was still incomplete, and dreaded another relapse—well knowing the frightful influence of the bad wife.

Some time after came the news that the man had beaten his wife and turned her out of doors. The adjutant went to see him. He said that a good life with that woman was impossible; but now that he was free of her he intended never again to fall, never again to drink, smoke, bet, or fight, but always to keep his soul pure and strong.

Here was a problem to begin with—the man's responsibility to his wife. Was he justified in turning her out of doors? Many will say Yes, angry that such a right should be questioned. The woman was bad, her influence checked the man's goodness, she stood between him and his God. But religious people whose logic is the commandment of an absolute Master cannot give that confident answer. This husband had promised to protect his wife—he had thrown her upon the streets. He had vowed before God to cherish her—he had abandoned her to the world. *His* salvation was a selfish salvation; without *hers* it was not the salvation of Christ.

And yet, to take her back, perhaps to sink with her down to the abyss—who could advise this dangerous course?

The adjutant, mothering the soul of this troubled man, was sorely puzzled by his problem; but the complexity of it was not yet reached.

He made his wife an allowance, they were properly separated, and he began a new life.

The change in him was really remarkable. He became smart in his appearance, clean in his habits, respectable in his way of living, and regular in his religion. He was never what one could call devout. His vision did not extend beyond the earth. The supreme influence in his soul was not celestial, but purely human; it was a desire to please the pure woman who had once appealed to his chivalry, and who had believed in him even when he lapsed again and again into sin. Through this humanity he reached into the religious sphere, so far as he was able.

The adjutant had to be content with this development of character, which seemed his utmost. She could not, being a woman, feel anything but pleasure at his devotion; she could not, being a missionary, prevent herself from feeling delight at the great change in his character; but, being a Salvationist, she remained disquieted by his distance from true spirituality, and anxious, always anxious, as to his future.

Some time had passed, and he was still a model of respectability in that foul neighbourhood, still an influence, at least for sobriety and order, in a quarter of the town where once he had been the ringleader in all things evil, when the devil once more got in his way.

Remember, that religion had changed him from a very bad man into a decent, sober, and self-respecting citizen; remember, also, that since the departure of his wife he had found it easier to maintain the battle against the pressing temptations of his neighbourhood—a really terribly difficult thing to do. Remember this, before you see him in his next stage. Converted, half converted, or not converted at all, this once quite bad man had become, under the influence of religion, a good man—for the neighbourhood in which he lived, a saint.

Well, this is what happened.

He rose early one morning, in his mother's lodging-house, washed, dressed, and set off before anyone was stirring for his daily work. As he opened the door, he saw the bowed figure of a woman crouched upon the steps under the porch. He took her for some poor old vagrant, who had stolen into that shelter for a night's lodging. He spoke to her briskly, but with kindness in his voice.

"Hullo!" he exclaimed, "what are you doing here?"

She lifted her face from her knees, turned her head, and looked up at him with weary, sleepy eyes. She was quite young. She was pretty. She was pathetic in her sorrow.

He saw that she was well dressed. He noticed that there was a black shadow under one of her eyes.

"My man struck me last night," she said, "and I left him. I'll never go back again."

" Your husband, you mean."

" No, he isn't my husband."

" What are you going to do? "

" I don't know. But I'll never go back to that one again."

" Well, I'm sorry for you."

" I shall do all right."

He felt in his pockets. " Look here," he said, giving her some coins, " you go and get yourself a cup of coffee. I'd do more for you if I could. Anyhow, I'm sorry. You're too young to be out in the streets."

He nodded to her and went off.

The adjutant says, not bitterly, and quite gently, that the devil entered into that girl on the doorstep. I rather think that the kind words of the man, and the masculine compassion in his attractive eyes, melted something in the heart of the poor forsaken creature and filled her with a new hope. Perhaps they were the kindest words she had ever heard. Perhaps the man was the best man she had ever set eyes upon. If one considers her position—the doorstep of a lodging-house on a bitter winter's morning, an entire loneliness in the midst of the great cold, unchar-itable world—and then endeavours to imagine the effect of kind words and compassionate eyes, there will be, I think, no need to drag in the agency of the devil to understand what followed. Remember that she was little more than a child.

The man came back from his work. The girl was waiting for him in the street. He had thought about her during the day. He was not sorry to see her there again. Something in her pretty face and pathetic eyes had appealed to him.

The girl stopped him, and spoke to him. They stood a few minutes in the street outside his home, talking together in low voices. He thought over what she had to say to him, and then they walked off together.

In a day or two the adjutant knew that this convert was keeping a mistress.

But here, to begin with, was a problem—he came as usual to the meetings in the hall, and maintained his religious bearing. Was he a hypocrite? One becomes impatient of such crude questions. Nevertheless, was it possible for the Army to countenance a man living in open sin? One great side of its work among the poor is for domestic purity. Very few people, perhaps, know how great a problem is presented to the social reformer in the slums by this vexed question of marriage. The Salvation Army has done, and is doing, an immense work for the sanctity of marriage. It has done, and is doing, this great work under conditions of heartbreaking difficulty. The law which permits husband and wife to separate without granting them that divorce which alone can enable them to marry again, has made for great immorality. Almost every man and woman so separated, thousands every year, find a mate and form a union unsanctioned by religion or State. The thousands, tens of thousands, of boys and girls who marry every year and then separate over poverty, drunkenness, or brutality, spread a vast influence over the community making for contempt of religious responsibility in the sacrament of marriage. The number of illicit unions in the poor quarters of London is extraordinarily great, and every year witnesses a further and wider weakening of the marriage bond. Against this deplorable condition of things—so dangerous to the State, so unhappy for posterity—the Salvation Army has opposed the strictest idea of purity. The most powerful weapon in its hand when combating misery and wretchedness is the shining testimony of the happy home, where religion consecrates the love of man and woman and creates the beauty of the family. The Army, working in the vilest parts of London, insists upon purity. No force, I really think, is doing more in the worst parts of England for the sacredness of marriage—on which so much depends—than this saving host of missionaries working by the ancient reed of conversion.

Well, what could the adjutant do in this matter? Was she to forbid the man to come to meetings, as the Church would assuredly forbid him her sacraments, and by so doing thrust him back

into his old excesses, his old lost state of depravity and sin? It was a difficult matter. One
course was open to her that seemed right and
hopeful, an appeal to his awakened conscience.

She saw him alone and spoke to him. At first
he denied the charge—anxious for the adjutant's
regard—then, when she smiled reproachfully, so
sad for that lie, and said that she knew the truth
—he protested that he was only standing between
the poor forsaken girl and the world that was
ready to ruin her. But the adjutant pressed her
charge with kindly and gentle sympathy, and at
last he looked her straight in the eyes and said,
" I won't deceive you; I care for her."

Then came the appeal to his awakened conscience, would he give her up? He was living
with her in sin, he was injuring her soul as well
as his own, he was not following Christ Who
had done so much for him, but was actually
turning his back upon that pure Saviour—would
he give her up? Help her to be good? Help his
own soul to be innocent and pure?

No; he would not give her up.

The man had reason on his side. The problem
lay in the sound reasonableness of his position.
He said the girl loved him purely, and helped him
to live a good life. He said that he had now
got, for the first time, a home that was happy.
He declared that without the love of this girl he
could not face the world. If she had dragged

him down, if she had made him indifferent to religion, he would have thrown her off. But, no; her influence was all for goodness, kindness, decency, respectability, and happiness. She was helping him. He could not see the crime or the sin of living with her. In his sin he had married a woman who dragged his soul to hell; in his regeneration he had found a woman who braced his strength for goodness. If the law freed him from his wife, he could marry this girl; if the law would not free him, he would stand by her, protect her, cherish her, love her to the hour of his death. No one should come between him and this good girl, who made him happy.

However reasonable this position, it was a position clean contrary to the injunctions of religion. From the point of view of the present world, the man's logic was unassailable. But religion looks to two worlds. What appears so unreasonable in Christianity is the logic which embraces the universe. Christianity is not a code of morals; it is a religion. It is not a terrestrial religion; it is a cosmical religion. For those who believe in it, all its injunctions, however hard and apparently unreasonable, are easy and just, because its purpose is the evolution and development of a spirit unbounded by time and place, and created for immortality.

The distressed and affectionate adjutant, confronted by this great problem, could only preach

her gospel, could only insist upon its insistence.
That insistence is emphatic enough. " Ye cannot
serve God and mammon." Professor James
speaks about " the divided self "; religion comes
to heal the division, to consummate a unity. A
hundred familiar phrases rise to one's mind.
" Thou madest us for Thyself, and our heart is
restless, until it repose in Thee." Empty thy
heart, says an old mystic, of all which may
" hinder that immediate Contact, that *Central
Touch* between thee and thy God." " The Per-
fection of the Soul is her union with God."
" What must the condition of those Wretched
Spirits be, who have no more union with God
than what is just enough to sustain them in Being . . . . what must the Darkness, what the
Poverty, what the Barrenness, what the Coldness,
Dryness, Deadness, Emptiness, Desolation, and
Solitude of such a State! *Depart from Me ye
Cursed!* I need not add into Everlasting Fire,
for here we have hell enough already."

It is religion which unifies the dual nature of
man, which saves him from the conflict by fixing
his purpose and his affection on one subject, his
Creator and his God. This is what mystics call
" the Unitive way of Religion." We must understand that position, before we can realize the
ability of such fine and compassionate natures as
those which follow Christ into the dark places
of our civilization, to preach an unequivocal gos-

pel to the sad and sorrowful for whom they feel
so profoundly.   One must perceive that these
people definitely and with a great assurance believe that no single soul can be happy, at peace
with itself, or secure in its evolution, which is
not united with the Will of God.   It is because
of this great assurance that they are so relentless
in their preaching of utter holiness.   Consider
for a moment these two striking testimonies:

" My sadness," says Adolphe Monod, " was
without limit, and having got entire possession of
me, it filled my life from the most indifferent
external acts to the most sacred thoughts, and
corrupted at their source my feelings, my judgment, and my happiness.   It was then that I
saw that to expect to put a stop to this disorder
by my reason and my will, which were themselves
diseased, would be to act like a blind man who
should pretend to correct one of his eyes by the
aid of the other equally blind one.   I had then
no resource save in *some influence from without.*
I remembered the promise of the Holy Ghost;
and what the positive declarations of the Gospel
had never succeeded in bringing home to me, I
learned at last from necessity, and believed, for
the first time in my life, in this promise, in the
only sense in which it answered the needs of my
soul, in that, namely, of a real, external, super-
natural action, capable of giving me thoughts,
and taking them away from me, and exerted on

me by a God as truly master of my heart as He is of the rest of nature. Renouncing then all merit, all strength, abandoning all my personal resources, and acknowledging no other title to His mercy than my own utter misery, I went home and threw myself on my knees, and prayed as I never yet prayed in my life. From this day onwards a new interior life began for me; not that my melancholy had disappeared, but it had lost its sting. Hope had entered into my heart, and once entered on the path, the God of Jesus Christ, to whom I then had learned to give myself up, little by little, did the rest."

"God," says Martin Luther, "is the God of the humble, the miserable, the oppressed, and the desperate, and of those that are brought even to nothing; and His nature is to give sight to the blind, to comfort the broken-hearted, to justify sinners, to save the very desperate and damned. Now that pernicious and pestilent opinion of man's own righteousness, which will not be a sinner, unclean, miserable, and damnable, but righteous and holy, suffereth not God to come to His own natural and proper work. Therefore, God must take that maul in hand (the law, I mean) to beat in pieces and bring to nothing this beast with her vain confidence, that she may so learn at length by her own misery that she is utterly forlorn and damned. But here lieth the difficulty, that when a man is terrified and cast

down, he is so little able to raise himself up
again, and say, ' Now I am bruised and afflicted
enough: now is the time of grace: now is the
time to hear Christ.' The foolishness of man's
heart is so great that then he rather seeketh to
himself more laws to satisfy his conscience. ' If
I live,' saith he, ' I will amend my life: I will
do this. I will do that.' But here, except thou
do the quite contrary, except thou send Moses
away with his law, and in these terrors and
anguish lay hold upon Christ Who died for thy
sins, look for no salvation. Thy cowl, thy shaven
crown, thy chastity, thy obedience, thy poverty,
thy works, thy merits? What shall all these do?
What shall the law of Moses avail? If I,
wretched and damnable sinner, through works
or merits could have loved the Son of God, and
so come to Him, what needed He to deliver Himself for me? If I, being a wretched and damned
sinner, could be redeemed by any other price,
what needed the Son of God to be given? But
because there was no other price, therefore He
delivered neither sheep, ox, gold, nor silver, but
even God Himself, entirely and wholly ' for me,'
even ' for me,' I say, a miserable, wretched sinner.
Now, therefore, I take comfort and apply this
to *myself*. And this manner of applying is the
very true force and power of faith. For He died
*not* to justify the righteous, but the *un*righteous,
and to make *them* the children of God."

Such is the faith of Salvationists, and such was the gospel, she had no other, which the little angel-adjutant of the slums had to preach to her convert. It is necessary for the reader to make himself well acquainted with the inexorable and unalterable gospel which the Salvationists insist upon with the lost and the evil.

He heard her out, did not attempt to controvert her arguments, and went away to live the life that seemed good in his own eyes.

She saw him several times, heard of him again and again, and never desisted from appealing to his better nature. But gradually he slipped out of religion, gradually he became less respectable, and at last he definitely—so it seemed—abandoned all struggle to be his highest.

The adjutant went to him in his home. The woman was not there. It was now the moment for her great appeal. With all the tenderness of her gentle character she made the man feel the difference in his present state and that of only a few months ago, when he was living in purity and serving God by trying to make other people better. He was softened, and in his relenting mood she pressed home to his heart the condition of the woman's soul with whom he was living in sin. Was she really good? Was she pure? Was she willing to live as God wanted all pure women to live—in service for others? Could he say solemnly before God that he was not preventing her by this life of sin from uniting her will with the will of God—from being her best possible?

He listened, wretched and unhappy, to her searching words. He knew their truth. Gradually this girl who had come to him like a spaniel, and who had seemed so sweet, affectionate, and pliant, had drifted into bad habits, had associated with women living a life like her own, was now hardening and growing dark of soul. The life was not a good one. But he was fond of her still. For him, there was no other woman in the world. What was he to do?

The Salvationist asked him to give her up, spoke about placing her in the Army's home for such women, made him hold the hope that one day this poor sinner might be herself rescuing the fallen and unfortunate.

He lifted his head at that. " I won't hinder you," he said. " I tell you what. I won't turn her out of doors, but if she goes, I won't go after her."

That was the extent of his sacrifice.

If it was not the utterance of one's idea of a converted soul, at least it was not very unlike some of St. Augustine's earlier prayers. How different, at any rate, from the thing he would have said before conversion.

An appeal to the woman succeeded, after much persuasion, in moving her heart towards renunciation.  She agreed to leave the man, and said she would go into the rescue home.

That very night the adjutant took her to London, carried her to the home, and remained with her till the next day.  But morning brought disillusion to the girl's mind.  She had not suffered remorse, she was not spiritual, for a cleansed mind and a pure soul she had no longing or desire. For the rest, the home did not appeal to her sympathies.  She had no broken and contrite spirit, such as that of the women in the place, most of them gladly content to work out their repentance in humility and silence and shadow.  The girl was not conscious of sin.  She would not stay.

So the adjutant was obliged to bring her back, and the girl returned to the man.

He was now lost to the Army.  He was, in technical phrase, a backslider.  The world might have pointed to him with amusement as an example of these emotional conversions.  Even the adjutant herself thought of him as a lost sheep.

No news of him came to the Salvation Army, he dropped out of that busy ministering life, he sank in the depths of the poor quarters, where religion apparently has no power.

And yet, hear the sequel.

The union was not happy.  Man and woman, sinking together, with no sacred affection to make them even kindly and forbearing to each other, quarrelled and came to blows.  They parted;

the woman to form another evil alliance, the man to take back his wife.

Long after this, the adjutant received her marching orders. A special service was organized for the night of her departure, a service of farewell to the best friend of the poor and the outcast who had ever worked in that town.

To her surprise the man attended this meeting, and at its conclusion he came to the penitent form.

Now there was no occasion for him to make this appearance, he derived no advantage by kneeling with the penitent, his attendance was his own will, his penitence—requiring no little courage— was entirely his own thought. One thinks that perhaps his failure to live the highest life was only a failure in relativity, that the adjutant's failure with her convert was apparent rather than real. For from this man she presently received a manly letter of good-bye, a letter which confessed his weakness, implored her forgiveness, and expressed his gratitude for her kindness— the letter of a backslider, but one whose sliding had not carried him right back. Is this not a case where one may attach a new meaning to a hackneyed phrase, and verily say, "'Tis better to have loved and lost, than never to have loved at all"?

The failures of the Salvation Army! What a book might be written of these people! However far they fall one cannot think that they ever forget the hour of their penitence, the moment of their vision, and the desire of their hearts for cleanness and mercy. In the larger self, that vast field of unexplored consciousness, the memory of these things works toward some end in their destiny, wholly good and wholly pure. A profound thought, deeply planted, can never be rooted from the mind, and a soul that has once looked and recognized and desired the highest can never for the rest of existence be perfectly satisfied with the lowest. One thinks that the failures pray in secret, some of them, and that nearly all of them—this I feel is really true and important to remember—never become so bad as they might have been.

> It's wiser being good than bad;
>   It's safer being meek than fierce:
> It's fitter being sane than mad.
>   My own hope is, a sun will pierce
> The thickest cloud earth ever stretched;
>   That, after Last, returns the First,
> Though a wide compass round be fetched;
>   That what began best, can't end worst,
> Nor what God blessed once, prove accurst!

# POSTSCRIPT

I THINK that every reader who brings an unprejudiced mind to the study of these narratives will feel and confess the wonder and the power of religion.

But scepticism will raise two objections.

We shall be told, first, that it is doubtful whether these conversions last; and, second, that the word religion is merely an unscientific term for mental excitement. The value of the conversions will be depreciated by the first criticism; their testimony to the truth of religion assailed by the second. I am anxious to meet these two objections which are so general in modern society, modern society with its mouth full of negations and its soul empty of affirmations, and to show their shallowness.

Most of the men whose stories are narrated in these pages have carried their regeneration over several years; not one of them has been recently converted. Such tremendous change lasting over a week, over a month, would be wonderful and worth while; what does scepticism say when all of these conversions are declared to be a matter

272

of years?  And here is a brief story of a man
converted by the Salvation Army long before it
had assumed its present form and title, while it
was still known among the polite as the Christian
Mission, and among the common people as the
Top-Hat Brigade, the story of a man who has
continued in his conversion, through difficulty and
obstruction, all those long years down to the
present day.

John Garry ran away from home at the age of
fourteen, and attached himself to a travelling
circus.  He is described as a " smart and wicked
brat, as good a boy at the game as you could
meet."  The immorality of this troupe did not
shock him in the least.  He proved himself as
cunning and impudent a rogue as ever lived a
vagabond life.  Ill-treated, badly fed, and over-
worked by his masters, he yet kept his audacity
and cheekiness, and saw that he got as much
pleasure as possible out of the general wickedness
of the company.  When he reached manhood he
was a dipsomaniac.  Turned away from circus
after circus, he took at last to a cadger's life, and
became what is called an " unemployable."  He
got drinks by performing tricks in public-houses,
such, for instance, as eating a cat.  For what is
called " a navvy's price," in other words, " a bob
and a pot," he undertook to eat any dead cat that
was brought to him in that bar, and the winning
of this wager established for him the name of

" The Cat Eater." He lived also largely by crime, and was always in hiding from the police.

Once, when he was sleeping in some bushes on a London common, he woke up to find a band of people gathered together beside a tent quite close to him. The men were in black coats and tall hats. The Cat Eater instantly imagined that they were detectives. When they saw him, spoke to him, and said that they were going to hold a religious service, inviting him to join them, he replied that if it were a job to nab him he would surely murder some of them. Still unconvinced by their assurances, he suffered himself to enter the tent, and there he was converted. He felt a desire for betterment. He prayed for mercy. He told the missionaries the story of his life, and said that he would begin again from that moment. They were kind to him, helped him to make a fresh start, and watched over his new birth. He married one of the women who had seen him in his rags and wretchedness kneeling as a penitent at that first meeting. And now, in his old age, he and his wife are prosperous and happy people, carrying on a good business in London, and following their religion with devotion. Never once through all these long years of incessant labour has the ex-dipsomaniac, the ex-cadger, the ex-unemployable, the ex-cat eater, looked back to his evil life.

Older, then, than the Salvation Army itself is

this conversion, and I could fill pages with similar stories. I ask the reader, who has not studied the question for himself, to believe my assurance that the records of conversion testify in an overwhelming percentage to lifelong victories. There is no question of that. And after all, as one endeavoured to point out in " Apparent Failure," the relapses among converted people only witness to the tremendous conflict in every man's soul between good and evil, only serve to make more vital an apprehension of this eternal duality in nature, only bring home to us the significance of this struggle, and the tremendous need for religion as a force in the conflict. Why the struggle to be good? Can materialism explain that? Why does religion convert at all? Can scepticism declare it?

But is it " religion "? Here we reach the second objection of sceptical people.

I want to point this out and to make it real, that however science may explain the psychological side of conversion, however convincingly it may show us that religion is a clumsy term for describing emotional excitement, science itself cannot and does not save the lost and rescue the abandoned. Science cannot do this; it knows how it is done, and yet cannot itself do the thing which it assures us is not a miracle; and science does not do it, does not desire to do it, for the very reason that it lacks the religious impulse which alone can accomplish the miracle, the miracle not only of converting people, but of making conversion of the evil and the bad a passion of the life of the good and the virtuous. It is really not so wonderful that religion should transform character and give new birth to personality as that it should inspire pure and holy people with a love for the degraded, the base, and the lost. That is, it seems to me, the great testimony of conversion, the love and the faith of those good and gentle souls who give their lives in rescuing the outcasts of society. Religion alone can create this sublime impulse.

A poor creature of my acquaintance, intellectually crippled and paralysed by success in the schools, endeavours to persuade me that there is no merit in this devotion and sacrifice of good people, because they like to do it, because they love doing it. And I in vain endeavour to make him perceive that unless they loved this work and were happy in it, there would be neither miracle nor merit. For is it not the most profound of Christ's revelations that all sacrifice of self and all labour for righteousness, without love, are of no avail? It is their love of saving souls which most testifies to the truth of religion. My poor critic, who never yet raised his finger to help a fallen creature, can charge good people with loving unselfish labour, but cannot explain how it is they come to love it. That is religion.

To the unprejudiced reader I offer this book, with the request that he will contemplate the narratives with honesty and common sense, considering within himself these simple reflections:

Men, radically bad, radically evil—a burden to the State, a scandal to civilization, and a disgrace to humanity—become, under the influence of religion, good, honest, industrious, and kind.

Homes where children suffer frightfully, where privation and tyranny obscure all the beauty and all the blessing of existence; homes so base, vile, and cruel that they cannot be described, become, under the influence of religion, happy, virtuous, and glad.

Vices which degrade men lower than the brutes, which make them loathsome in the sight of respectable people, and fill our prisons and workhouses with an immense burden on the community, under the influence of religion lose every fibre of their power, and drop away from the strangled souls of their victims like dead ivy, like an outworn garment.

Sins and crimes which retard the progress of the race, which breed corruption, degeneration, and prosperous misery, under the influence of religion cease to have power over the minds of men, and in the instant of conversion appear horrible and inimical.

Let the reader bear these things in mind, and ask himself what would become of humanity if materialism triumphed over religion, and life were revealed to the masses of the human race only as a struggle for existence. Could the law, could eugenics, assure us of evolution? " Socrates confessed that it was through a hard struggle that he attained virtue. An ultra-evolutionist would have eliminated him in his first stage. Nero, on the other hand, set out well." Professor Goldwin Smith, who makes this telling remark, might have cited with Socrates the great Augustine, St. Francis, David, and many another whose struggle towards righteousness has sustained and assisted generation after generation of men struggling to attain their highest. Hear him on the necessity, even from a material point of view, for religion in its sanction of the conscience:

" But if this life ends all, I do not see how conscience can retain its authority. The authority of conscience, it seems to me, is religious. . . . In the absence of such a sanction what can there be to prevent a man from following his own inclinations, good or bad, beneficent or murderous, so long as he keeps within the pale of the law, or manages to escape the police? One man is a lamb by nature, another is a tiger. Why is not the tiger as well as the lamb to follow his nature, so far as the law will let him or as he has power? Eccelino, for instance, was by nature a devil incarnate, a sort of Satanic enthusiast of evil. What had merely utilitarian morality to say against his gratification of his propensities as long as he had power on his side?"

The common sense of this subject is that life without conscience becomes a destroying animalism, and that conscience without religion has neither force nor justification for its restraints.

Those who know life deeply and intimately, who are profoundly acquainted with all the suffering, sorrow, misery, and sin of cities and villages, those whose studies are not limited to books read in a library, or to discussions accidentally started in a drawing-room, know as the first axiom of their knowledge that religion alone among all the forces at work for the improvement of humanity has power to alter the character and regenerate the soul of evil people. Legislation may better house the poor, may educate their children, limit the opportunities for drink and crime, and punish evil-doers with a saner and more determined effort at their moral reformation, but without religion they will never give spiritual joy and rejoicing strength to the posterity on which evolution depends.

"No heart is pure that is not passionate; no virtue is safe that is not enthusiastic."

When I visit the happy homes and experience the gentleness, kindness, and refinement of such people as those whose life-stories appear in this book, and compare them with the squalor and misery of the great majority of homes surround-

ing them, I am astonished that the world should
be so incredulous about religion, and that legisla-
tion should be so foolish as to attempt to do
laboriously by enactments, clumsy and slow, what
might be done instantly and easily by religion,
if it had the full force of the community at its
back.

Greater faith is necessary to the salvation of
this country. Without God, vain is the work
of the builders.

ing them, I am astonished that the world should be so incredulous about religion, and that legisla-tion should be so foolish as to attempt to do laboriously by enactments, clumsy and slow, what might be done instantly and easily by religion, if it had the full force of the community at its back.

Greater faith is necessary to the salvation of this country. Without God, vain is the work of the builders.